HOMESTEADING FOR BEGINNERS

How to Start Homesteading From Scratch

TABLE OF CONTENTS

INTRODUCTION

To get by every day, a person is required to earn a salary. With this salary, they can buy whatever they need; be it food, comforts, or saving for a brighter future. However, to get this salary, many people are stuck in dead-end jobs, grinding away hours of their lives to afford what they believe they need. For others, a single salary is all that stands between them and being on the street. Is this the life you strive for, or do you dream of something more? Many people believe this is just the way of life, but it isn't. What if I told you there was another way? There is a way you can secure a roof over your head and put food on the table. All you need to do is work the land. This is the art of homesteading.

WHY CHOOSE HOMESTEADING?

Every year, more and more people are turning to homesteads as a way to avoid the stress of living and working in the city. Why is this? Homesteading is the act of living a self-sufficient life while limiting as many outside factors as possible. A person who turns to homesteading wants to be as self-sufficient as possible. However, before you sell off everything you have and start looking for a plot of land to work on, realize that homesteading requires a lot of hard work. It isn't something that many people are capable of or brave enough to follow through with. Homesteading has a steep learning curve, and when you aren't suitably prepared, your homestead is likely to fail early in your attempt.

Despite homesteading being a difficult activity to start, it is very fulfilling, as it offers you more freedom than a 9–5 job ever could. It allows you the freedom to choose what you decide to grow, raise, and sell. By being in charge of growing your own food, you know that what you put in is exactly what you get out. It further ensures a healthier way of eating while also educating you about where food comes from.

By choosing to live a self-sufficient life, you are lowering your carbon footprint and considering your health. Were humans truly meant to spend hours in cubicles or in front of computers? No! We're meant to be out in nature, reaping the benefits of working the soil and not buying every new gadget that hits the market. One of the first things you will need to learn about homesteading is that you don't need to buy things to make you happy. Happiness is simpler than that.

Homesteading teaches you to be independent, how to rely on yourself, and what nature can throw at you. By developing skills that allow for self-sufficiency, you gain the abilities to repair, build, and preserve food, and the list goes on. The main thing that holds people back from making the leap is fear. This is the fear of the unknown, the same fear you feel when you prepare for a job interview or an unexpected life event. This fear can easily be banished by understanding the steps needed to make the intentional move away from your current norm.

HOW TO MAKE THE MOVE

Homesteading has as many ups and downs as living in the city, except it is quieter and therefore, calmer. Moving to a homestead away from where you live should be done gradually. It takes time to research the laws surrounding homesteading and what's expected of you and your family. If your partner and children aren't willing to make the move, you may find this more of a stressful situation than a calm one.

The first thing you need to do is plan out what you want to achieve. Planning starts with research, so get a notebook and a pen handy to jot down a few ideas as you go through this book. Start with a list of things you think you may need. Then do research into what is needed on a homestead. I guarantee that it is more than what you expected.

Know what you want from your homestead. Are you escaping the city, or are you trying to lower your carbon footprint? Determine the types of goals you want to achieve. Divide them into long-term and short-term goals. Then think about how you want to achieve these goals. You will need the support of your family and friends but realize that not everyone will understand your need to start a homestead. You will likely be met with ridicule or scoffs. These will change quickly enough when you bring a freshly made pie where all the ingredients were grown by you.

Consider the location of where you want to live, and what laws may have an impact on what you want to do with the land you get. The further this property is away from conveniences such as stores, doctors, and schools, the more prepared you will have to be. The land itself will affect what you can and can't grow over time.

Gain knowledge from those who are already living the lifestyle. This is just one book of many that are out there to help you reach your goal of owning your own homestead. What they will all emphasize though is that you will need to learn how to make a dollar stretch further than you ever thought possible.

PREPARATION

This isn't an overnight adventure. It takes time to prepare what you need on paper, and then it takes time to get the funds. Very few people can make the move to a homestead within a few short weeks. The preparation you put into your homestead should also be extended to preparing your self-sufficiency skills.

Join a Community Support Agriculture (CSA) group to help you prepare yourself for what is expected of a self-sufficient lifestyle. These groups are a collection of people and farms that work together on a piece of land, sharing the work, responsibility, and the bounty which is reaped. They also teach you the benefit of having a community and relying on your neighbors when you need help. These are also the people who you can turn to to get ideas for moving to a homestead.

Don't have a CSA? Then turn to backyard gardening as a way to grow some of your food. Raised beds, vertical gardening, and container gardens are a perfect way to prepare yourself for what is to come with larger-scale gardening on your homestead. If your bylaws allow it, add a few chickens to your garden to deal with pesky insects that threaten your harvest.

Educate yourself on how to preserve what you grow. Sometimes the harvest is such that you cannot hope to eat all of it, and you don't want it to go to waste. There are many ways to preserve all manner of food.

One of the biggest changes you will have to prepare for is making your money last longer. Unless you are still planning to drive from your homestead to your day job for the rest of your life, there is a chance you won't be getting as big of a salary. Yet, this won't matter as you won't be buying many things once you have your homestead established. That doesn't mean you can become complacent and waste money. While you are still living in your urban retreat, look to learn how to budget and save where you can. On the homestead, there will be no one else to mend your clothes or fix tools. By learning to do these yourself, you learn valuable skills and manage to save a few dollars.

ABOUT THIS BOOK

Homesteading doesn't start on the homestead; it starts in your home right now! *Homesteading for Beginners: How to Start Homesteading From Scratch* is a beginner's guide to everything you need to know about homesteading. Page through this vault of knowledge as you learn how to garden to provide for your family, look after your chosen livestock, and even perform basic first aid in an emergency. By carefully planning what you want to grow every year, you can even save money by making natural remedies for ailments that see most people reaching for over-the-counter medicines or rushing to the emergency room.

Take charge of your life right now and learn how to make the move from your current life to the life of a homesteader. Homesteading life isn't for everyone, but anyone can give it a try.

CHAPTER 1: GETTING STARTED

While preparing the homestead, you need to consider where you want your homestead to be. While urban homesteaders can practice their skills from their own homes, others may want to move away and live a more secluded homesteading lifestyle. Regardless of which you want to try, there are a myriad of laws that need to be followed in terms of water, electricity, waste removal, zoning, and building codes. To add to the confusion, no one state has the same laws as the other, while some county laws trump state laws.

Laws Around Homesteading

Many laws will influence your homesteading lifestyle, so it will require a lot of research on your part to determine which is the best place for you to call homesteading paradise. It isn't illegal to have a homestead in any of the US's states, but some laws can restrict what you can and can't do on the property. These laws are generally determined by the area's local government, which means each area you look at may have vastly different laws that can affect you.

That said, some states are better than others when it comes to homesteading. According to Diane Vucković (2022), the following states are the worst to have a homestead in:

State	Laws
Nevada	**Electricity** • The state requires permits to be off g **Water** • The state has a harsh climate. • You're allowed to only harvest rainwa single-family home's roof. • Only non-potable use for water colle **Waste** • There is strict regulation on alternativ systems.
Utah	**Electricity** • The use of off-grid solar power is leg **Water** • The state restricts rainwater harvesti • With a permit, 2,500 gallons may be • Without a permit, no more than two may be collected. **Waste** • Primitive outhouses are illegal.
Colorado	**Electricity** • Some counties require a homestead the electricity grid.

	Water
	    • Very strict on water gathering.
	    • Only 2 rain barrels with a combined ᵥ
	may be collected.
	    • Only non-potable use for water colle
	Waste
	    • Most homes may be required to still
	municipal sewage system for wastewateɾ
	    • Compost toilets are legal.

Maryland	**Electricity**
	    • Off-grid solar systems are allowed w
	inspections.
	Water
	    • Some local laws force homesteaderₛ
	the municipal water supply.
	    • Some counties offer incentives to co
	potable uses.
	Waste
	    • Compost toilets are legal.
	    • Off-grid septic tanks are illegal.

Pennsylvania	**Electricity**
	    • It's illegal not to be connected to the
	grid.
	Water
	    • It's legal to harvest rainwater.
	Waste
	    • Has strict rules about outhouses and
	    • Homesteads will need to have a
	connected to the municipal sewage systɛ

New York	**Electricity**
	    • Off-grid solar systems are illegal in ɱ
	Water
	    • Wet plumbing is required in all new ᵇ
	    • Some areas allow homes to be discɔ
	municipal water with permits.
	Waste
	    • Compost toilets are legal.

	• You'll need to be connected to the m system to deal with wastewater.

New Jersey	**Electricity**
	    • Allows for off-grid solar systems, but
	the local building codes.
	Water
	    • May collect rainwater.
	    • Only non-potable use for water colle
	Waste
	    • Many places don't allow off-grid was
	    • Off-grid toilets are legal but highly re

Rhode Island	**Electricity**
	    • The state does have incentives for p
	powered.
	    • No home may be without power, son
	remain connected to the electrical systen
	Water
	    • Some places force you to remain on
	system, while others allow you to collect
	below ground.
	    • Potable water that comes into the ho
	pressure.
	Waste
	    • You must be connected to the munic
	wastewater.
	    • Compost toilets are allowed, but onc
	cleaned the waste should be disposed of

Connecticut	**Electricity**
	    • The state promotes people having of
	Water
	    • It's legal to collect water and be disc
	water utility.
	Waste
	    • Compost toilets are legal but have to
	submitted and approved by the local dire

Massachusett s	**Electricity**

	• It's legal to be off-grid, but it's illegal ⸱ power. **Water** • Rainwater may be collected. • Only non-potable use for water colle⟨ • Some counties don't allow for privat℮ **Waste** • Some places require you to be conn⟨ sewage system. • Other places allow compost toilets w

These are just an overview of the worst states identified. To get more information, you will need to investigate what's required by the county laws where you will be living. If you are unsure about the laws, speak to fellow homesteaders in the area to get a rough idea of what is allowed and what isn't.

Other laws you will need to consider are zoning laws. A piece of land is set aside for a particular purpose and is zoned for that purpose. However, not all land has zoning laws. This is a double-edged sword. While a piece of land with no zoning laws has fewer regulations than those with zoning laws, this doesn't mean they don't have any regulations. This needs to be followed up on before the land is purchased. The last thing you want is a piece of land that allows you to build whatever you want but won't allow you to park your recreational vehicle (RV) on the property to live in while building your home. Know what is and isn't regulated.

Another law you need to be concerned about is building codes. You must know the local building codes before you decide to put anything on the property you own. It would be a waste of time and money to build a home only to find it isn't up to code, and you need to destroy it or spend a fortune trying to bring it up to code. This protects you in the long run from possible lawsuits.

What you build and bring onto the property to live in will also be determined if you need permits, have to abide by certain regulations, or if it needs to be inspected. Although many people believe cabins circumvent this issue, it doesn't when it is your permanent residence—although this may be dependent on where you live.

Building a home on a homestead takes time. Many people like to do it over weekends while still living in the city. This means they tend to buy RVs which sit on the property but are only temporary residences. Some counties don't allow for this, while others allow them to be temporary or even permanent residences.

Something that will help you get your property up to standard is getting a certificate of occupancy. This will prove that your property abides all laws, and if it isn't, you can get guidance on how to bring it up to standard. You will need to research what you need in each state to get this certificate.

When considering using solar power, where legal, it may even help you earn money as some states will buy back excessive power through net metering. However, others may charge you. Be wary and do your research. In areas that don't allow you to fully leave the electricity grid, consider making use of the microgrid laws. This allows you to have a system in place to generate power (solar panels, wind turbines, or even geothermal wells) even when the main utility is down.

Many people who move to a homestead dream of fresh produce and products they can make and then enjoy. Others dream of making some money off of these fresh treasures. Indeed, this is a great way for your homestead to make money for you. However, this too is a double-edged sword as there are laws you should abide by to ensure your products are safe for others to consume. You may need permits and licenses to sell certain items (unpasteurized milk or honey), add labels on any goods you make, and may even need to have inspections on your property to ensure you are working in sterile conditions.

Declaration Of Homestead

Living on a homestead is hard work, and even when you pour all of your passion into it, there is a chance that things go wrong. Crops may die in a drought, diseases may ravage your livestock, and you can accumulate debt. To protect your homestead from creditors, you should get a homestead declaration. This form—filed with the county recorder's office—protects the homestead from creditors being paid from the proceeds of your homestead in case of your untimely death.

There are some rules surrounding this, such as how much money is owed, if the property was put up as collateral, or if a lien was placed on the property due to non-payment after improvements were done to it.

Each state has its unique version of this declaration—such as the Massachusetts Homestead Act—so you'll need to research what is needed by your particular area to get one. Contact your county clerk to see what you need to do to ensure the safety of your homestead, especially if you have a partner and children. The last thing you want is for all your hard work to be lost due to a year of bad luck.

What You Need

Now that the overview of the laws is out of the way, we can concentrate on what you need to make your homestead the home you deserve. When making a list of what is necessary, consider what you need to survive. The three essentials are shelter, water, and food. A fourth can be added to the mix, and that is energy. Once you have a way to get those, it is only a matter of keeping them stable so that you can live a comfortable life.

Property

Your property is the most important part of your homestead. You want a piece of land that not only you can live on, but that can support you in every way. It needs good soil for planting, natural resources (trees, streams, foraging opportunities, etc.), and as secluded as you want it to be. Be wary of being too secluded, as this will impact the time it takes any emergency services to reach you when something goes wrong. This property will be influenced by the hardiness zones, weather, and wild animals. So, select it carefully if you want to avoid yearly natural disasters or hungry predators.

Once you have a rough idea of what you want from your homestead, identify where you want to live. As discussed earlier, some states are more difficult to have a homestead in than others. When you have decided on the perfect place, search online or real estate listings for available properties. Can you purchase the land outright, or do you need a loan from the bank? If a loan is required, go to the bank and see what you qualify for. A preapproval for a loan will allow you to see how much you can spend on your dream homestead.

Even if you do find the perfect piece of land, you need to do some more sleuthing. You might find the perfect piece of property but may not have access to everything that is on it. Review the deed of the property to ensure you have mineral and water rights to what you want to purchase. If you are lucky enough to have a well on the land, ensure that it hasn't been contaminated, is well maintained, and is in working order. Any land that has restrictions on it will hamper your ability to live the way you want to.

Size

The size of the homestead is vital. Too small and it won't support you, too large and you won't manage to handle it alone. For a large family and several types of livestock, five acres is more than enough to support you in terms of food and space. This space needs to be divided into where you will live (RV camper, cabin, etc.), your garden (less fertile ground means you need more space to grow in), orchard (if you want fruit trees), livestock grazing area and their shelter, and space for any future projects you may want to complete. If you find the urban homesteading lifestyle more appealing than the full homesteading lifestyle, you don't need more than a tenth of an acre to farm in.

Other things you need to consider when choosing the right-sized property are your skill level and how ambitious you are. Be wary of biting off more than you can chew when starting. It's a good idea to start small and grow rather than starting large and allowing projects to fall to the wayside.

Next, consider how much you are willing to pay for your ideal parcel of land. It is rare to find land for free, but it isn't impossible, especially if you are willing to go to Alaska. While you are in your research phase of homesteading, take the time to figure out your expectations and goals.

Food

Getting to grow your own food is practically the whole point of becoming self-sufficient for many homesteaders. However, this can be near impossible if you choose the wrong place to settle. To have the best productivity from your property you need to consider:

- hardiness zone
- climate and conditions of the county
- weather patterns
- microclimate on your property
- soil characteristics (type, pH, and fertility)

You must know what your hardiness zone is, as this will affect what and when you can plant. The higher the hardiness zone, the longer you can grow, but some cold-loving plants may not grow to their best. When the climate is particularly bad, you'll need to consider ways to protect your crops as they grow. This can be done with greenhouses, hoop houses, or even growing indoors. However, this can drive up the cost of your homestead as you'd have to purchase the necessary items to farm in this manner. Areas that have high temperatures will result in you needing more water.

Poor soil will make it difficult to get a good harvest. Take several samples of soil throughout the property you are interested in and have it tested. Not only will this allow you to determine the fertility of the soil, but it will also help to identify what type of soil you have, and its pH. Most vegetables prefer a slightly acidic to neutral soil which is high in organic matter. Even if the soil is poor, you can get fertilizer—or you can make compost —and work it into the soil.

An average person needs 2,000–2,500 calories a day, though this is subject to activity levels and body conditions. This means every person on your homestead will need upwards of 900,000 calories a year to feel comfortable (Greg, 2021). To get this number of calories, you will need a minimum of 0.2–0.4 acres of gardening space to produce vegetables and grains for a family of 4–8. If you want to grow animal feed, you will need even more space.

The amount of food you generate will depend on what you grow. Some plants are once-off (radishes), while there are plants that produce throughout the season, such as peppers or tomatoes. You can even invest in a small orchard of 12–15 fruit trees, which measures to roughly half an acre. The only problem is that the trees need time to mature to the point where they give the volume of fruit needed to be sustainable to you. They should be started early on the homestead as young saplings instead of trying to grow from seed.

Your garden will need to be south facing —or north facing in the southern hemisphere—to reap the benefits of the sunlight. Vegetables that make fruits (tomatoes, peppers, squashes, etc.) all need a minimum of six hours of sunlight, while leafy vegetables need a little less. This can comfortably tide over a family of vegans, but if you are an omnivorous or vegetarian family, you may need to include animals or animal byproducts to be added to your diet.

When considering livestock, remember that they too need the same essentials as you do to survive. Animals come with pros and cons. They offer protection against pests (ducks love slugs), their manure can be used as compost and depending on what animal you have, and you can get a variety of products from them without needing to slaughter them. However, they can get into your garden and destroy it, get ill and injured, and each type will need to be managed differently in terms of space and food. Animal feed is another vital component to consider, as it can be grown or bought depending on your allotted budget.

Shelter

You and any livestock should be sheltered from the elements and possible dangers. What shelter you build or drive onto the property needs to follow all zoning and building codes of the area. The size of the shelters is determined by the number of animals or people who will occupy them. While shelter for humans can be pretty cookie-cutter, different animals need different kinds of shelters to be comfortable.

Spacing within the home will also be dependent on the ages of the people living in it. Younger children don't need as much space as an adult. Your home may also need to incorporate workspaces, common areas, and even studying areas, depending on your goals and needs.

Energy Requirements

While some homesteaders prefer to partially remain on the grid; many others want to try and get off most of the grids. If your goal is to go off-grid you will need to produce your own energy. To do this successfully, space is required. The more items you need to power in your home, the more space you will need to use to produce the energy needed. There are a variety of ways to produce reliable renewable energy.

Solar energy is generally relied on because it's easy to calculate the power generated through the formula: hours of sunshine multiplied by the solar panel wattage. Yet it isn't just about how to generate energy, it's about being able to store it. Regardless of how you generate energy, you'll need deep cycling batteries to use when you can't make your own power. You don't even need to limit yourself to solar power. If your land is conducive to it, consider using wind or water to power turbines to charge batteries—especially when the sunshine is weak.

The energy you generate will do more than just power your electrical items, it will also help to cool or heat your house if you so desire. If this is the case, you will need to work out if you can afford that heater during winter, or air conditioner during summer. This is where you can use natural resources to aid in keeping the temperatures comfortable regardless of the time of the year.

There is no need to rely on electricity to keep your house warm or cool. How you build or position your home can allow a throughflow of air that can cool it at the height of summer. To heat your home, consider a fireplace or a wood stove. A wood stove will also allow you to cook your meals.

An average urban home uses roughly 850 kilowatt-hours (kWh) a year (Greg, 2021). Luckily, you will not have to generate this amount of power on your homestead as you'll likely not have as many electronic devices. It's wise to teach yourself to be more frugal with your power. This way, you can always have power in an emergency. How much energy you want to generate is dependent on the space available for your power-generating means, i.e., the size of the roof used for solar panels.

Miscellaneous

Here are a few more items you will need to consider when choosing your property. Consider the remoteness. There is no reason to live in the middle of nowhere to be a homesteader. It's about being self-sufficient, not being a hermit. You should still be a part of a community that can help you if things go array. Have a neighbor close enough to offer a hand in case of an emergency. Don't be too far away that medical help can't reach you. Accidents happen, and the longer it takes for help to get to you, the worse the result may be.

Check the zoning laws if you want to have livestock! If you want them to graze, you will need to allocate a piece of your property to allow this. You will also need to consider the zoning of the adjacent plots surrounding you. Some may share the same water source (possibility of damming), allow hunting (danger to your livestock), use herbicides and pesticides (potentially contaminate your crops and animals), or may be zoned for industrial use.

You will also need to consider road access to your property. This not only makes it easier to get in and out of your property but will need to be maintained. This means needing a tractor to clear the road if it becomes damaged or snowed under.

While researching the area you want to get a piece of land in, look out for potential hazards that could affect you.

This includes predators, pests, environmental disasters, and contaminated water sources.

Thanks to modern technology, remaining connected to the internet is possible. In some cases, it is easier than others. Check to see if the property has access to a phone line or internet. It's more than just being connected to the outside world. It's about opening another way to make money, either through doing your work remotely or selling what you make on the homestead.

Natural Resources

The property you decide on should have some natural resources you can use. These can help buffer some of the costs and other materials you use on your homestead.

Wood

Having woodland on your property will be a great boon to you. If it's a coppiced woodland or forest, even better! Cutting back the brush encourages fresh growth for the new season, and you get the wood required to aid in heating your home. An acre or two of woodland isn't necessary, but a bonus if you can find a property with it. You can even use trees as material to construct your home, shelters for animals, or fencing.

Water

Having water delivered to a rural area is costly both in time and money. A stream or well on the property is important. However, you will need to ensure these are reliable sources of water—surface and groundwater—throughout the year and not just seasonal. Supplement natural water resources with rain collection and storage of water where you can. You can even remain attached to the grid's water and sewage lines.

How much water you need can be difficult to calculate as it will depend on the climate, the size, and needs of your garden, livestock needs, and human needs. An average human requires about half a gallon of drinking water a day but will need more depending on their activity levels and body condition. Then you need to consider items in the homes that require water such as toilets, dishwashers, and baths or showers. In the developed world a person can use as much as 40 gallons of water every day with everything they do (Greg, 2021). This means a single person can power through roughly 15,000 gallons of water a year. Thankfully, there are a variety of ways you can be frugal with your usage of water. This can be achieved by installing low-flow flushing toilets or switching to showers only.

Where you can't save water is when you need to water your animals and garden. The hotter the environment, the more water you will need. Larger gardens and animals will require more water than smaller varieties. Some plants are more water-hungry than others, so you must research what you want to grow before planting anything in the ground.

Tools

Most of the tools you will need when starting your homestead, you may already have in your possession. So, before you go out and start buying tools, consult this nifty table to see if there is anything you may need beyond what you already own.

Use	Tools
Land clearing and development	**Gardening** Shovels (round and square), broad leaf rake), broad fork post hole digger, hoses, ((temperature tells you if you the compost), and hoes. **Harvesting** Fruit pickers (great for tree: baskets (space to add harvest gallon drums (storage or conta **Cutting wood** Axes (splitting firewood and trees down), splitting wedge, loading wood), and can't ho logs). **Heavy lifting** Wheelbarrow, utility trailer (nee a vehicle), and lawn tractor (p pull utility trailer).
Construction and carpentry	**Hand tools** Tape measure, hand or speed 4-foot level, sledgehamme handsaw, paddle bits, file (for i grit), hole saws, and a T-squ straight edge on sheet wall). **Power tools** Drill (battery operated is fine, run out of power at the wor chainsaw (constructing cabi saw.

	Extras Ear protection (against chai~~leads.~~
Maintenance	A basic set of screwdrivers (full set of wrenches and socl plus deep well sockets), r sockets with extensions and pliers (needle nose, wire strip vice grip, etc.), tie wire, duct ta
Miscellaneous	Generators (emergency pow charging battery packs), sma good quality knife, and multit you).

Homestead Specific Equipment

When it comes to tools, sometimes you need something to help with the heavy workloads on your homestead. Some tools are more needed than others. The below table lists equipment that will benefit you in the long run.

Equipment	Use
Rear tine rotary tiller	• Helps prepare the ground to ready for planting. • Can be used in place of a plow • Can overheat if it becomes c roots.
Come-along	• A hand-held winch and ratche between two posts. • A wire fence mandrel can be help keep the wire around the post 1
Tractor	• Most expensive tool you'll buy. • Fulfills many roles, such as p be used to lift tree trunks and move
Harvester	• Only necessary if you gro\ sunflowers, or soybeans.

	• This harvests these crops far fa hand.

You may find that your homestead needs more or fewer tools. At the end of the day, what you purchase is up to your discretion. If a tool has a function that will help to live on your homestead easier, then it's worth investing in it. When buying tools, always go with the best quality that your pocket can afford.

Preparing The Property

Once you have your dream piece of land, you'll need to prepare it. You will need to decide where to place your house, garden, and pens for livestock if you want livestock. As different livestock have different requirements, they'll be discussed further in Chapter 4.

Homes

Depending on the zoning and building laws in your area, you are spoiled for choice when it comes to what you can live in. Many first-time homesteaders tend to take their time establishing their homestead and will live on the property several days out of the month to prepare the land or build their homes. A RV is great in terms of space mobility. Some can even be outfitted to run on alternative power sources. They can even make a comfortable home for two people if you have no interest in building on your property.

Another moveable home you can consider—although it can be a little pricey at about $90,000—is an Ecocapsule. This tiny camper is run on solar and wind power and can even gather rainwater to run the internal plumbing. It's a comfortable fit for two people with a kitchen, dining room, bathroom, and bedroom.

If you are aiming for something larger for a family, you will need to consider building or buying a premade home. Micro cabins can be built to your specifications, plus you can add to them as the years go by. Alternatively, you can look at an off-grid cabin that is premade. These homes get delivered as different parts which are assembled in the area where you want to place them.

If you are a little more ambitious, build an Earthship home. These large homes are designed to be self-sufficient, off-grid living spaces. They're built to get the most out of the natural heat generated by the sun and ground, harvest rainwater, and function well on solar energy.

There are other temporary homes you can design and build, including cob and straw bale homes. Use what materials are readily available to you before you purchase anything. You may be surprised what you can use to build your home.

When building a home, you don't want a house too large to heat or keep cool. Ultimately, the homesteading life is one of minimalism. You don't need extra rooms or space to store stuff, as everything you own will have a function at some point on your property. You'll also need to consider where you place your home. A south-facing home is great during winter but can become sweltering at the height of summer. More on that in Chapter 2.

Electricity

Some people like to remain on the grid but have a backup system ready in case the main grid fails. Others like to leave the grid completely. Whatever you want, have a look at your property to see which of the alternate natural energies you can use.

Solar Powered

Solar power is the most popular of the alternate energies. It's easy to calculate the amount of power you can receive from the solar panels (photovoltaic panels) depending on the duration of sunlight. Another pro is that solar panels can be placed on most flat surfaces, such as roofs. However, they do have their downsides. The startup can be expensive, and you only have so many hours of daylight that you can use—and these will diminish the closer you get to winter.

A solar power system generally consists of the panels, a charge controller (charges batteries till they are full), batteries (stores power), and an inverter (changes direct current to alternating current). These can be sold as kits or separate if you want to design a unique system.

The first thing you need to do before purchasing anything is to quantify your electricity needs. There isn't an endless supply of electricity on your homestead, as from the grid. But how much should you be generating? You will need to select the electronics that will be running on your homestead and work out how much each device draws and how much it will use over time. Some electronic devices draw power constantly, while others don't. To see what the various devices are draining your power you can get a meter that can read what they draw and how much they use over 24 hours. These meters—such as the product Kill a Watt meter—can be plugged between the device and the power supply. The first reading you get will be how much the device draws; make a note. After about 24 hours you can determine how much it uses over time.

Once you have done this with all the devices you deem necessary, you will need to calculate the energy needs for your off-grid home. The total you get will determine the size of the inverter you need to purchase. A 1,000-watt inverter will allow you to run enough devices that require a combined power amount of no more than 1,000 watts.

For this amount of power to be generated, you need a certain duration of sunlight. This is dependent on the weather, where you are, and the time of the year. You can find your sunlight hours online, so you don't need to calculate them. With the duration of sunshine and the number of watts you need, you can work out how many solar panels you need to power your home. It is always a good idea to get 1–2 panels more than what you need to make up for poor weather days. This can also help to charge batteries quicker.

Many vendors can help you design a solar system once you tell them roughly where you live and your energy needs. Shop around and get many quotes before settling on what you want to buy.

Wind Powered

It is generally a good idea not to rely on a single type of renewable energy. Solar power cannot be generated at night. However, wind power can be harvested. Wind turbines can generate energy no matter when, as long as there is a wind blowing. Its setup is similar to solar power, but instead of solar panels, you will have blades that catch the wind and spin to generate power.

The best place to install wind turbines is at the highest point of your property. For some, this may even be on top of your home. You will then need to determine your average wind speed for your area. Don't take the county average as wind speed is influenced by the topography and the microclimate on your property.

There are some cons to using wind turbines. They have more moving parts, so it'll need more maintenance. Wind turbines can get quite large—as seen with windmills—but the larger the turbine, the larger the rotor needed to turn the blades. These can get surprisingly large, and not everyone has a place on their property to place a windmill. Luckily, there are small varieties that can sit on your roof and generate just enough energy to recharge your batteries of the power you use during the night. There are many designs to choose from.

Water Powered

A running stream or river close to your home is ideal for generating power. Hydroelectric power is more constant than either sun or wind, and depending on how cold it gets, it can continue throughout the year. Hydroelectric works similarly to a wind turbine, but the turbine is powered as water runs across its blades. The remaining components to charge batteries and create alternating current are the same as the previously discussed alternative energies.

Although this seems to be the best fit out of the three, its initial startup is expensive, the wiring needs to be isolated from the water, and getting the power to your home may involve long stretches of power cables when the water source is far away.

Others

There are other ways to generate energy —such as geothermal energy—but this requires a lot of money and being in a specific area where the heat of the earth can be used. Regardless of which way you want to generate power, you'll need to find ways to lower your power usage to save as much electricity as possible for things that are needed.

One of the ways you can save on using electricity is through passive living. When designing your home, consider what materials you will use to build it. Some materials can trap heat, while others reflect it. Something as simple as painting your roof a darker color will help it to absorb more heat.

Southern-facing homes heat well during winter but can get hot during summer. Combat this by adding thicker or darker curtains to all rooms that face south. Alternatively, when building your home, position it in such a way that opening a few windows creates a natural path for a breeze to pull through the house.

Regardless of how you generate electricity, you need to treat it the same way you treat your money. As long as you have money, you can spend it. Once it is gone, you can't do anything. It's the same with electricity. Use it sparingly, and always have a backup in place in case you need to work on your main power system.

Water

This is an essential which won't necessarily be available on your homestead. Perhaps this is because laws prevent you from collecting rainwater, or you don't have access to the water rights on the property. If this is the case with where you live, you will need to consider having water delivered. Even if you have some form of natural water on your property, such as a well, you may find you have to supplement what you need through a water delivery. When considering a property like this, you'll need to determine if you can have bulk water delivered to your homestead. Sadly, this will take a chunk of the money you need to put toward your homestead. Take a long look at your water needs and then decide whether a property with no water or water rights is worth the effort and money you will have to put into it.

Rain

Depending on where you live, rain is a free water resource and is considered the cleanest of the water sources—before it hits a surface. However, not all states allow for rainwater harvesting. Utah and Colorado are very strict about how much water you can harvest from rain. But why? In the case of Colorado, it is a century-old law that prevents the collection of rainwater as it can have an impact on water reaching someone else downstream. Yet it isn't only these states that have an issue with the harvesting of rainwater freely.

State	Conditions
Colorado	Only allows for 110 gallons to be collected in rain t
Idaho	Allows for the collection of rain that lands on roo not harvest rainwater that has entered a waterway
New Mexico	Requires a permit for rainwater harvesting system:
Ohio	Has multiple codes and regulations to uphold th harvesting.
Oregon	May only harvest from rooftops.
Utah	Requires a permit to harvest rainwater up to 2,500

Despite these being state laws, county laws may differ, so be sure to check what you are allowed to do in your area.

When in an area that allows rainwater harvesting, you can easily calculate how much you can harvest per year on average. Per square foot of roof surface, you can gather roughly 0.6 gallons of water per inch of rain that falls. There may be some wastage as raindrops bounce from the roof surface. This water then runs into the gutters and can then be deviated into barrels or tanks with a system of pipes. The best roofs to collect water from are metal or tile, slanted roofs. Never collect water from asphalt roofs.

It is generally not a good idea to drink water collected from your roof directly as it can be contaminated with anything that happens to land on it. However, this water is perfect for the garden! If you want to drink this water, you need to put it through a filtration and cleaning system to make it consumption friendly.

Groundwater

To determine if you have potential groundwater, check the United States Geological Survey (USGS) to see if you are over any underwater aquifers. When in an area that has groundwater, you can have a well dug, if allowed. However, this can be costly as you will need to hire professionals to do surveys of where the best locations will be to drill. There is also a chance that the first time you drill, you don't hit water, and the deeper you drill, the more expensive it will become. Preferably you want a well close to your home, not close to a road, your animals, or any farming equipment.

The average well depth is about 150 feet and can cost several thousand dollars. It is expensive, but it is a small price to pay for a near-constant supply of water. As long as the water table doesn't drop—which can occur during droughts—you should have water for as long as you are on the property.

Even if you do find water, there is a chance it is unusable. Underground water can be contaminated with hydrogen sulfide or arsenic—and only one has a telltale smell. Any water from a well needs to be tested to ensure it is safe for human, plant, and animal consumption. Even if a well is safe to drink from, before you can pump water from it, you will need to have a filtration system in place and possibly a treatment plan if you have hard water (which contains calcium and magnesium).

As a well is drilled, a casing is lowered, protecting the well from collapsing. Once you have hit water, you can add a pump with a sand filter. This will prevent sand from getting into the pump and your faucets. Pumps are required if you want water from the well to where you want it. For shallow wells, a hand pump can be used, but for longer wells, you will need to resort to either an electric pump— remember to add its energy requirement to your calculations for electricity—or a solar pump.

Once a well is in place, it can last for decades, while the pumps will burn out quicker. It requires little maintenance. A well can easily become contaminated by external factors such as fracking, earthquakes, or drilling. An animal falling into a well will also foul the water and potentially make you sick. Cover the well opening with a mesh covering to prevent this from happening. If your water starts to smell and you can't find a reason for it, have it tested.

Springs

Springs are naturally occurring wells. Water bubbles up through the cracks of the Earth's surface from groundwater sources. They are rare, but if it's on your property with water rights, you can use it as you want. Some springs are stronger than others, so it isn't a source of water you should rely on for permanent water. They can often disappear during droughts or even a single hot summer. Depending on the size of the spring you have, you can deviate the water to the waiting water tanks.

Surface Water

Other potential surface water available on your property includes rivers, lakes, and ponds. You can only use these sources if you have water rights. If you have the rights, you are entitled to pump some of the water from the source to your waiting tanks. However, you will not be allowed to dam or deviate the course of streams and rivers, as this will affect neighbors further downstream.

Gathering Water

Unlike rainwater that can be collected close to your home, well and surface water needs to be transported to your home. Pumps need to bring that water to areas where you will store it until you are ready to use it. Cisterns (water tanks) can be placed above or below ground, the location you choose is determined by whether you want to use gravity or not to feed water into your home. These tanks are usually made of plastic, but you may find others made of fiberglass, concrete, or even metal.

Pumps used to gather water from wells and other resources, depend heavily on the size of the pipes used to pump from the source. Choose a pump that matches the diameter of the pipe (or well shaft), gives you the flow you need (gallons per minute), and won't burn through your power reserves when using an electrical pump.

Tanks situated higher than the house can use the force of gravity to create the water pressure needed within the pipes of the home. Alternatively, you will need to use pressurized tanks and pumps to get the pressure required. To determine what kind of pump you need to get water into your home, you need to calculate the capacity of the water needed. This means looking at the number of fixtures you have and what kind of pressure you want the water to flow out at. Once you know what you want, you can get the pump which will give you the volume per minute to ensure the pressure you want.

As the pressurized cisterns fill with water, they compress what air is in the tanks. The pressure you want to exert on the water can be set on a pressurized tank. As the water is used, the air pressure on the remaining water in the tanks is less, and this is where the pump will take over for the pressure you require in your home.

Cleaning Water

No matter how clean the water looks, you can never assume it is safe for consumption, even if tests show it is free of heavy metals. Any water used for consumption and bathing should be filtered and treated. When planning to have running water in your home, it is best to add inline filters, as this will clean your water as it travels through the plumbing. They can be a little tricky to install, but it is worth it when you have running water. Cisterns will also need cleaning now and again. Some bleach to the water in the cisterns will ensure your water is drinkable. The volume of how much bleach is determined by the volume of your cistern.

However, not everyone wants running water in their homes. It takes time to install, and pipes need to be looked after during freezing winters. Luckily, there are other options available. A gravity-fed filtration system can be used to filter water through different filtration levels, using gravity. Once the water reaches the bottom of the filter, it should be safe enough to drink. This can be installed in your home, or in areas where your livestock will drink. There are many brands on the market. What you decide to get is up to your needs.

Sewage

Talking about sewage is the least glamorous part of living on a homestead, but it needs to be done. While animal waste can be used as compost, the same cannot be said for all human waste. While the contents of a compost toilet can be composted to be used as fertilizer, it can take about a year to ensure the bacteria and other microbes are killed. Even then, human waste fertilizer should never be used on annuals, only on trees and shrubs.

There are two types of human waste: greywater and blackwater. Greywater is water waste generated when people clean themselves (baths or showers) and any water used to clean (sinks, washing machines, etc.). Blackwater is used water that contains human waste such as fecal matter, urine, and even vomit. These are loose definitions, as greywater also tends to contain human waste such as skin cells. Each type of waste has its own way of being dealt with.

There is nothing wrong with greywater if you aren't using harsh cleaning agents or disinfectants. Greywater can be used for a wide variety of functions, such as watering the garden or flushing your water-dependent toilets. This wastewater needs to run off into a holding tank designed for greywater. From here, the wastewater can be directed back to where you want to use it.

The cheapest and easiest way to deal with blackwater waste is to invest in a compost toilet. These toilets can be as simple as a large bucket—rimmed with something like a pool noodle for comfort —with sawdust or a specifically designed toilet, which can be pricey. These toilets require no water and can be relatively odorless when used correctly. To use this toilet, the bottom of the bucket should have a four-inch layer of sawdust before use. After each use, the waste should be covered enough so the next person doesn't have to see it—about an inch of sawdust is enough. Toilet paper can be added to a compost toilet. The only issue with this kind of toilet is that if there is too much moisture it can cause more of a smell. To avoid this, add more sawdust or swap the buckets frequently, and remove the waste, following the law set out by the county.

There are two more ways you can deal with this waste, if you have flushing toilets, and that is either through a lagoon or a septic tank. Ensure that you are legally allowed to have either before you consider them.

A lagoon is used when the soil on the homestead isn't an effective filter as is needed with a septic tank. Wastewater runs from the homestead into a pit far from where people or animals may encounter it. This open sewage pit will, over time, through microbial action, break down the waste in it. This is the cheaper alternative to a septic tank but has multiple drawbacks. It requires more space, needs to be further from your home and property line, and will pose a health risk if not managed correctly. It should also be fenced off to prevent anything from stumbling into it.

When allowed on properties, septic tanks are one of the most common methods of dealing with all wastewater. The septic tank is buried on the property. It has pipes that lead the wastewater from the home to the tank through an inlet pipe. As the wastewater fills the tank, the bacteria which occur naturally in human waste start to break down the solid materials anaerobically. This causes the wastewater to be separated into a solid sludge, a liquid component, and scum (oils, fats, anything that shouldn't go down the drain) which floats on the surface. As the liquid reaches the opening of the outlet pipe it travels down the pipe toward a distribution box. This box will direct the liquid to a series of perforated pipes in the leaching (drain) field. From here, the liquid will percolate out of the pipes into the surrounding soil —allowing any bacteria remaining in the liquid to be distributed and eaten by the soil microbes. The filtered water will eventually return to an underground water catchment area. A septic tank should only be placed in an area where the soil allows for the filtration of the liquid waste. Soils with high clay content will need to be removed and replaced with sandy or loamy soil. This soil will then need to stand still for up to a year before the tank and leach field can be added.

Septic tanks come with a few manhole covers, and these shouldn't be covered after burying the tank. It's through these holes that the tank will need to be cleaned every 3-5 years. When deciding to place a septic tank, be aware that you may be required to have a septic permit even before you get a building permit. Contact your general county government offices to get more details about what you can and can't do in terms of placing a septic tank.

Installing a Septic Tank

Installing a septic tank is a big job. It is likely best you hire someone to do it for you as they will have the necessary tools and equipment to handle everything. However, if you're confident enough, and are hiring heavy lifting equipment to do other jobs on the homestead, then you can install the septic tank yourself. Remember, a septic tank and its leach field need to be inspected before it is covered up. Depending on your county's laws, you may even need a plumber to connect your household plumbing to the septic tank.

Septic tanks need to be a minimum of five feet away from homes, though some people prefer them to be ten feet away; in case they want to expand something on their home. Septic tank sizes depend on how many chambers they have, and how many people will be using the plumbing. A family of four will need a septic tank with a capacity of roughly 1,000 gallons. The dimensions of the tank will differ as they can be rectangular or cylindrical.

Once you know the capacity you need for you and your family, you can shop around for a septic tank. When placing the tank, be sure the hole is deep enough to cover the tank and for it to be level. An unleveled tank will cause problems in the future.

The area where you want to place the leach field needs to have all trees and brush removed before you can start. This field needs to be a minimum distance of 20 feet from the home, and 100 feet away from any wells. Even the septic tank shouldn't be within 50 feet of a well, in case of contamination were something to go wrong with the tank.

When digging the leaching field, it needs to be about 3–4 feet deep for each 100– 150 feet of perforated pipes, each of which should be separated by 1–3 feet. Ideally, when digging the trenches, you want about 6-12 inches of gravel under the pipe. Then you want to cover the pipes with landscaping fabric—this will prevent soil from getting into the holes— and add another two inches of gravel over the pipes. Then you want to add 18–

30 inches of soil, but never less than 6 inches, and level the ground out. The pipes in the leach field can be looped to connect or capped at the end, whatever design best suits the ground you can dig in. If in your digging, you encounter bedrock before reaching the prerequisite depth, you may need to move your leach field somewhere else. Bedrock can breach the surface somewhere on your property and bring you and your animals into contact with any waste liquid traveling along it.

Septic tanks and the leaching field shouldn't have any heavy traffic over them as this can lead to damage over time. It is in your best interest to have these areas marked out.

CHAPTER 3: GROWING YOUR OWN FOOD

Having a garden is wonderful. It allows you to not only be creative but allows you to grow your food the way you want to. It all starts with a plan before you put a single seed in the ground. Expect problems and mistakes to happen when you start. A garden needs more than just sunlight and water. A well-designed garden requires foresight and effort. The plants may grow by themselves, but you manage their growth. They need to be cared for so you and your livestock can be fed.

How To Make A Garden

Before you get all excited about growing a giant crop, stop for a minute and think. How long do some plants grow? What can I expect from a certain crop? Gardening is equal parts research and work. If you aren't going to do the research, you are going to do a whole lot more work!

Where your garden will be located is your first job. You want the area to get as much sun as possible. This may require you to do some work around that section of land to remove trees that cast shadows at some point during the day. A southward-facing garden is best in the northern hemisphere. Consider how tall the different plants will grow. Tall plants such as wheat or corn, or trellised plants such as beans or peas, need to be placed more to the northern part of the garden to prevent them from overshadowing any plants growing more to the south.

Sunlight doesn't stay in one place throughout the year. The winter sun may not shine in the exact place as the summer sun. As the seasons change, you can determine what you need to go with your garden. You may even want to design separate gardens to deal with the different seasons. This will also allow the ground to rest in between planting.

Consider the consistency of your soil. Not all soils are perfect and may require you to till them while adding compost to give your garden all the nutrients it needs. You don't even need to consider tilling in your first year. It may be easier to use no-tilling but rather added compost and mulch on top of the soil to grow your plants in. Mulch plays an essential role in preventing the soil from drying out and certain pest species getting to your crops. Then, when you are ready for the following season of growth, you can work the already added compost into the soil. The choice is yours whether you want to continue with non-tilling or not.

Regardless of what method you want to use, the ground needs to be cleared of any wild brush, weeds, and trees before you can start working the land. This may take some time, so get friends and family to help you.

Buying compost can put a dent in your budget. So as soon as you're producing organic waste on your farm (animal waste, kitchen scraps, etc.) you should make compost. Good quality compost can be made within 6–8 weeks if you know how, but it can take up to a year to get the right consistency. Quality compost needs to reach a high enough temperature to kill off any diseases and bacteria that may come along with the waste. With enough time and care, the waste turns into a dark brown to black, earthy-smelling organic matter. If the compost smells terrible, it has likely gotten too wet, and anaerobic bacteria are rampant. This can be fixed by turning the compost, allowing it to get more air and starting the composting process again.

A combination of compost and fertilizer is necessary for soil that has never been gardened before. It returns much-needed nutrients and elements (nitrogen, phosphorus, and potassium) into the soil. While compost can be used freely, fertilizer should be used sparingly. The instructions on the fertilizer need to be followed carefully to avoid plants' foliage (leaves) and roots suffering from fertilizer burn.

Carefully consider what you want to grow. You want high-yielding, fast-growing plants, but you also want to grow what you like to eat or can trade away. This is where being neighborly can help you. You can strike a deal with a neighbor to grow something in exchange for something they grow on their farm. However, choosing a suitable plant isn't as easy as picking something from a seed catalog. You should consider how long it takes for a plant to reach maturity. There are different hardiness zones throughout America, and these zones create a set growing season. The lower zones will have a shorter growing season than the higher zones. This growing season gets interrupted by frost—except in Zones 10–

13. Not many plants are resistant to frost and will likely die.

Even if you are in a zone with a short growing season, you can gain a few weeks of growing by planting transfers (seedlings) instead of seeds. Some plants have a preference for different zones. Ensure what you decide to grow can survive outside of your zone. To determine your hardiness zone, use the United States Department of Agriculture (USDA) Plant Hardiness Map. Then get a plant calendar that matches your zone. This calendar, sometimes known as a farmer's almanac, will tell you when the best times are to grow certain plants.

To thrive, gardens need a steady supply of water. How this water is delivered is up to you. Some homesteaders are happy to use a hose, while others install homemade drip irrigation systems. When considering an irrigation system, ensure it can easily be removed when it comes time to till the land.

When planting seeds, you need to read the catalogs or packets carefully. Not all seeds are equal. Ideally, you want to get heirloom seeds, as these carry strong genetic lines that will have a stable production. If these are heirloom seeds produced in the area where your homestead is, you can be assured that they will thrive well. From the heirloom plants, you can collect seeds for the next growing season, saving you from buying new seeds for a new crop.

Many people may be enticed by the promises of large yields when it comes to hybrid seeds, but it is a double-edged sword! The first generation from the seeds will match what was promised. However, because they are hybrids, once they create new seeds, the different genetic lines will split between the various seeds harvested. This leads the next generation not to have all the benefits the first generation had. The plants may look different, produce different yields, and have no consistency.

When deciding between seeds and transplants, you will need to consider the pros and cons. Transplants are a guaranteed plant, and they save you weeks of growth. However, if you are buying them, there isn't a wide variety. Seeds are hardier to frost than transfers, and you have a wider variety of plants to grow. However, a seed doesn't guarantee a plant.

One of the deciding factors of what you grow is the yield. Radishes are delicious, but a single seed only gives one radish, while a single cucumber seed can give many fruits. Try to find a trade-off between what you like to eat, high yield, and once-off plants. Don't only think of fruits and vegetables! Consider herbs. Many of the woody herbs—mint, rosemary, and thyme—are perennial in mild climates and annuals in areas where there is frost. If you want these herbs to survive the winter, add them to pots and bring them indoors or in sheltered areas.

Once you have decided what to grow, you will need to decide how to grow those particular plants. Some plants like to climb or sprawl. This wastes a lot of space you could be using to grow other plants in. Consider adding some trellises for these plants to free up space but still get a large yield. Growing your plants in rows makes it easier to see what is happening in your garden. You can even mark out specific areas for certain plants, so you know what is sprouting. A wise gardener never plants all the seeds they have at one time. This results in a mass of crops all ripening at the same time, meaning you will be picking, preserving, and trading more than what you can handle. Stagger planting seeds, so that you have crops ripening throughout the whole season.

Each plant has its own needs. Some prefer a certain soil type, while others prefer more water. All have their preferred depths and distances they want to be planted from their neighbor. All this information can be found on seed packets or in catalogs.

Yes, plants need water, but they also need air. Plants that are both too close together and are being watered too frequently—especially on their foliage—welcome fungal infections such as powdery mildew and rust. Plants should never be soaked; the soil should be moist at best.

Even once your garden is flourishing, you can't leave it alone. It's a colorful dinner plate waiting for something to come along and eat it, and many animals are willing to answer that call. Insects and weeds are some of your smaller pests, but there are larger animals such as deer, rabbits, and raccoons. All are more than happy to take what they need. *You must find a way to protect your crops from pest animals.* While fences that extend above ground can control deer, you will need one that extends below ground to deal with rabbits. Fencing can be made with wood or metal; it comes down to what you have and what you're willing to buy. You will also need to explore alternative deterrents to keep pests at bay. Think of getting some dogs to deal with large pests, and cats to handle rodents.

To control weeds and insects there are a variety of ways for you to remain on top. Firstly, there is the use of herbicides and pesticides. These are poisons and need to be handled with care. Their instructions should be followed to the letter. Read the instruction pamphlet to determine if they can or should be used on your homestead. If you prefer having an organic garden, there are many natural deterrents for insects that won't kill your beneficial types. As for the weeds, well, you'll just have to get weeding. Mulch can help suppress weed growth, but too much can also suppress the growth of your crops. Take the time to recognize what your intended seedlings look like, so you don't accidentally weed them out.

Gardening is by trial and error, and the longer you are growing your own food, the quicker you notice what will work and what won't. Keep a handy planting notebook. Make notes about what plants thrive while others fail. If you intend to try crop rotation, you can draw detailed maps of plant positions within your garden. This ensures you never grow the same plants in the same area year after year—draining the soil of its nutrients.

Consider Hydroponics

Don't discredit the use of hydroponics on a homestead. The only vegetables that cannot be grown in a hydroponic setup are root vegetables. Hydroponics is a soil-less growing setup that has a nutrient solution added to the water to allow the plants to get all the nutrients they need. The plants are anchored in a non-fertile medium—such as gravel—to prevent them from falling into the water, while their roots are submerged. This farming method can even be combined with aquaponics if you are so inclined.

So why consider hydroponics? Perhaps you have a small piece of property, and you want to supplement your food. Hydroponics is perfect for growing indoors during winter, and most setups don't require much space. This is one way to overcome poor soil that needs time to become nutrient-rich again. Plants such as tomatoes have been known to grow faster and produce larger yields when grown in a hydroponic system

(Advanced Nutrients, 2019). There is less chance of pests and soil-borne diseases affecting your crops. Plus—despite using water throughout the system—you save water as it isn't being absorbed by the surrounding area or being affected by evaporation as much.

The typical—and easiest hydroponic setup—is the Deep Water Culture (DWC). You'll need an area large enough to grow what you want to. Then, you will need:

- tanks that can hold the water
- Styrofoam sheets with holes cut out for your plants
- plants of choice in containers with gravel, vermiculite, or perlite
- air pumps to push air through the airline tubes
- airstones to oxygenate the water

If the area where your hydroponics setup isn't sunny enough, you may have to invest in some grow lights for your plants to get the necessary sunlight. There are some drawbacks to a hydroponic system. Firstly, you cannot easily grow plants from seeds, as you need an established root system. Secondly, if you have many systems working simultaneously, they tend to draw a lot of power. You'll have to calculate whether a hydroponic system can work on your current electrical grid.

What To Grow

Below you will find a list of the easiest plants you can grow on a homestead. However, don't feel limited to this list as there are a wide variety of plants you can grow and enjoy. Give these plants a try while you're still living in an urban setting to give yourself the best possible chance of knowing what to do once you're on your homestead.

Plant	Type	Benefit
Tomatoes	Fruit	• There are a wide ra and sizes. • Has a high yield per s • These fruits are e preserved. • One of the easiest fru • The plant doesn't i grow when trellised.
Squashes	Fruit	• There is a wide range varieties. • Some can take up t are packed full of vitamins • Seeds can be saved • Winter squashes ha\ them to be stored for se cellar. Summer squash stored for long periods. • These are vining pla lot of space. They can ç strong trellis, but the fru prevent them from breakir
Red raspberries	Berry fruit	• This plant only nee and requires minimal care • It can be grown alor manipulated to grow as a a natural windbreak.

		• When planting a yc need to be soaked for a being added to a hole acc • Not only are the fruit can be used in a tea bones and helps with mer
Carrots	Root vegetable	• This vegetable requ develop the edible root. way will cause it to grow s • There are many color tasty, whether cooked varieties can even be grov • The greens are just a • If the soil of the hc consider growing this veg
Radishes	Root vegetable	• There is only one and that is it's a once-off v • It's one of the fastest it matures within 30 radishes, ensure you sta you don't want too many r • There are a wide sizes. • Great raw, cooked, c greens make a great pe salads. • This is a cool-loving grown from spring to the don't plant at the height cause the plants to bolt— • Radishes don't like nitrogen. Soil should be r cause the bulb to crack.
Corn	Grain	• There is a wide v cultivars. • As tall plants, these s northern section of your s

		• The ears can be ea[...] either human or animal c[...] • The best corn to gro[...] heirloom varieties. • This plant is a heav[...] of nitrogen from the soil—[...] with legumes. • Corn grows best with
Cabbages	Leafy vegetable	• There are many col[...] varieties. • These vegetables are[...] like direct sunlight. • They enjoy nitrogen-[...] benefit when planted aft[...] worked into the soil. • The leaves can be e[...] fermented. • These plants are [...] slugs.
Peanuts	Legume	• Not a nut at all, but [...] to fix nitrogen to the soil. • This crop grows u[...] best in tropical areas b[...] Zone 6. • Needs direct su[...] harvest. • Be wary of potential [...] • Can be eaten raw, bo[...]
Peas	Legume	• With its fragrant flow[...] for producing delicio[...] attracting pollinators to yo[...] • Peas prefer soil with [...] • As with all legumes, [...] fixer. • These plants come [...] and bush cultivars. Som[...]

		within their pods, while shelled before eating. • The climbing variety \ a trellis. However, when stalks can be used as trel
Parsley	Herb	• Don't forget to cc They can benefit your he your garden. • Parsley makes a gre it attracts predatory wa many kinds of caterpillars • This plant needs optimum. • It hates to compete \ to weed well around them

Soil condition and weather play a significant role in whether certain plants will survive to maturity on your homestead. Some plants are just tricky to grow—such as bulb onions or Brussels sprouts—in comparison to others. Your garden needs to work efficiently to produce as much food as possible, without you breaking your back trying to make it work. If a type of plant requires too much effort, water, or money to grow, it isn't worth growing.

A person needs roughly 160–200 pounds of vegetables and fruit a year. To get a rough idea of the yield of your crops, consult your seed catalog—many of which can be found online for free. From here, you can calculate what other fruits and vegetables you need to grow to meet the expectations of your preferred diet.

When planting an orchard, know that many fruit trees need several years to reach the stage of producing a reliable crop. These trees need a lot of sunlight and care to reach this stage. It's a good idea to start your orchard within the first year of being on your homestead. Grow a mixture of regular and dwarf varieties to get fruit production starting as early as 2–3 years. Raising a tree from a sapling instead of a seed saves a lot of time.

The main thing to remember about your garden is that you are growing for yourself and not the wider market. Don't be surprised that your crops don't look as perfect as the images in the seed catalogs. Even if they look a little funny, they still contain the nutrients you need. Finally, don't expect a perfect yield every year, many things can influence it. *Keep taking notes every year to help with the following season.*

Growing Feed

Some homesteaders want to offset the cost of animal feed (pellets, hay, and alfalfa), so they plant their own. When cleaning the orchard and garden, the waste such as stalks, vines, and clippings can go to the animals instead of the composting area. However, before giving any of the livestock plants you have grown, you need to check if it is something the animal can eat without problems. Plant residue from potatoes and onions isn't great for all animals.

Depending on the number of animals, you may need to dedicate as much as 1–2 acres to grow their feed. Here are a few ideas of vegetables you can feed your livestock.

Crops	Instructions
Corn	• Corn can be grown to maturity befor(animals such as cattle, pigs, poultry, and g(• Alternatively, once the ears have bee(can be moved into the area to clear the res • Corn can also be grown as a foraging r 70–90 days of growth, cattle should be all(trim the plants. They shouldn't be allowed than three inches above the ground before gives the forageable crop time to recove cattle to feed again. However, allowing cause them to wander into your garden t crops. Ensure you have sturdy fencing to pi • Be wary of feeding sweetcorn to rumil with multiple stomachs such as cattle, go: can cause bloat and diarrhea.
Squashes	• Animals such as sheep, goats, cattle, love pumpkins and squashes as an occasic • Winter squashes store well into winte animals when all other crops cease to grow • Squashes should be broken open or c feeding them to animals.
Carrots	• The whole, raw vegetable can be giver goats, and poultry.

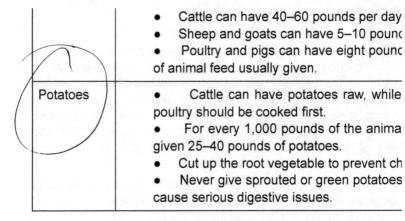	• Cattle can have 40–60 pounds per day • Sheep and goats can have 5–10 pounc • Poultry and pigs can have eight pounc of animal feed usually given.
Potatoes	• Cattle can have potatoes raw, while poultry should be cooked first. • For every 1,000 pounds of the anima given 25–40 pounds of potatoes. • Cut up the root vegetable to prevent ch • Never give sprouted or green potatoes cause serious digestive issues.

Keep in mind that feeding your livestock these vegetables should only be a supplement to their main feed, such as hay or alfalfa. Most commercial animal feed is specially formulated to have the correct protein, carbohydrates, fats, and nutrients for that particular animal. Deviating from their needs can result in illness, failure to thrive and produce eggs and milk, and can even cause reproductive issues. Consult a farm veterinarian about supplementing your livestock's food to ensure they get as good a quality meal as what you would expect for yourself.

Getting the Best Yield

To get the best possible yield is more than just growing plants that provide more fruit and vegetables per plant. It is about how different plants can help each other to get the best yield possible. They do this by adding nutrients to the ground, warding off pests, and attracting beneficial insects.

Companion Planting

Companion planting is a theory that many people believe, despite all the evidence being anecdotal. The theory is that certain plants that grow close can benefit each other in some way. This can be through a variety of different ways. Companion planting isn't a new strategy. The Three Sister planting strategy was perfected by the Native Americans.

By growing corn, beans, and squash together, each plant benefits the other. The beans provide more nitrogen to the soil. The corn grows tall, allowing the beans to use their stalks as a trellis system. There is also ample space between the corn stalks, allowing the squash to spread out around them. The squash's large leaves shelter the ground below, preventing it from drying. They are also covered in prickles, which act as a tactile defense against some pest species such as raccoons.

Not all plants grown together are good for each other. Some companions secrete chemicals that actively discourage the growth of other plants. While some can actively kill other plants through chemicals (allelopathy), generally, poor companions will only result in smaller plants. This occurs in peas when grown too close to alliums (plants from the onion family). Neither of these plants will thrive, but they will still grow. Below are some examples of good or bad companions for beginner-friendly crops.

Plant	Good Companions	Bad
Tomatoes	Basil, carrots, lettuce, and peppers.	Corn, potato from the cabl
Squashes	Corn, lettuce, melons, and peppers.	Any brassica
Red raspberries	Any of the alliums, such as chives, garlic, and onions.	Eggplants, po
Carrots	Brassicas, garlic, leeks, and peppers.	Dill, fennel, a
Radishes	Beans, cucumber, lettuce, and peas.	Any other roc

Corn	Beans, cucumber, dill, melons, and peas.	Any brassica
Cabbages	Beans, beets, carrots, potatoes, and Swiss chard.	Peppers, squ
Peanuts	Lettuce, radishes, and snow peas.	Corn, fennel,
Peas	Beans, carrots, spinach, and strawberries.	Any alliums.
Parsley	Chives, peas, and tomatoes.	Carrots, lettu

Another reason certain plants shouldn't be grown together is that they share too many of the same pests and diseases, as seen with parsley and carrots.

Although many herbs give a wide array of benefits, not all of them will be good for garden use. Everyone loves the smell of mint, and it is perfect for tea, but it is a nightmare when it grows loose in a garden. Mint is an aggressive grower and spreads as readily through its root system as its seeds. It doesn't take long before it takes over your entire garden. If you want mint in your garden, contain it in a pot, where it can't spread anywhere else.

You don't need to only combine fruits and vegetables; consider herbs and flowers to aid in many functions. Flowers such as nasturtiums, marigold, and borage are perfect to attract pollinators and other beneficial insects to your garden. You will need as many pollinators as possible, as the more they pollinate, the more crops you will have.

Plants can be divided into self-fertile—where the flower can be fertilized by itself—and plants that require a pollinator. Plants such as tomatoes, cauliflower, and onions are considered self-fertile, while plants such as melons, berries, and cucumbers aren't. You will need flowers to attract pollinators to help these plants make fruit.

Natural Pest Control

Pest control starts with what you plant, not what you spray. Planting crops such as onions are known deterrents for some insects, but not all of them. As chili peppers grow, they release a chemical through their roots that aids in fighting microbes that cause root rot in many other plants. The French marigold is great for deterring whitefly. However, you need the roots to remain in the soil after cutting back the flower at the end of its growing season, as this deters root-knot nematodes.

Planting herbs not only gives you another crop to utilize, but many attract beneficial insects that are predators or parasitoids —insects that parasitize other insects and eggs. Basil, sage, and dill are perfect for attracting lacewings, ladybugs, and parasitoid wasps. Parasitoid wasps will take care of many caterpillars and aphids, which are some of the most damaging species in your garden.

You can even consider growing trap crops—also known as sacrificial crops—to attract pests away from your main food source. Nasturtiums act as a trap crop for aphids and cabbage worms. They are so palatable to these pests that they eventually become completely infested. Once this occurs, remove the plant and destroy it to prevent the spread of pests.

The best way to get all the benefits from insect deterrent and trap crops is to grow them between your other plants. You will still need to monitor your crops now and again to see if nature is balancing itself, or if you need to step in.

In case you are forced to step in but don't want to use insecticides, consider some more organic poisons to deal with your problems.

Organic Pesticides	Information
Bacillus thuringiensis (Bt)	• This is a soil-borne bacteria has been long used as a natural i • This bacterium is sprayed on and then consumed by insects contact with the pH of the stoma and causes damage to the digesti

	• Together with the toxin the the damage caused to the dige stops eating within hours and dies • Different strains of Bt affect s a good idea to match the strain to • Bt is effective against most and butterflies), while some strai gnats, flies, and beetles.
Neem oil	• The active ingredient in ne which disrupts the insects' ability t • It also affects the hormona ability of the insect to mature enou • Neem oil is a medium to broa that affects most orders of insects • Insects need to feed on it to acts as a deterrent. • This poison works well on a and diamondback moths.
Pyrethrins	• Pyrethrins are commonly insecticide sprays used in homes. • This toxin is found in many co chrysanthemums. • It needs to be applied dir poison affects their nervous syst paralysis followed by death. • Works on all insects.
Spinosad	• This poison is made by soil-li • It affects a wide range of pes arachnids (red spider mites) to thr • All pests that come into co the poison are affected by it. • The affected insect starts muscles before paralysis sets in. day or two.

Insects not only eat your crops, but they can also spread many kinds of diseases. However, this isn't the only way disease is spread. There are a wide range of soil-borne bacteria that can devastate your garden. Applying mulch will prevent splashing back against your plants when you water them. It's best to aim water close to the soil, so you don't get the foliage too wet, as this can spread fungal infections.

Keep a close eye on your crops, and you'll notice when something is amiss. When the foliage changes to an odd color, it may be a sign of a disease spreading. Remove affected areas of the plant—or the whole plant—and destroy them. Never compost diseased plant matter. Lastly, clean your gardening tools regularly. There is no quicker way to spread disease to other parts of your garden than with contaminated tools.

Saving Seed

As a beginner, you should consider saving seeds to use for the next growing season. Saving seeds may not be an easy task for all plants you want to grow, as some are easier to harvest and store than others. With some practice, it does get easier. So, while you are a beginner, why not try saving some of the self-fertile plants such as tomatoes, peppers, beans, or peas? These plants give fruit with seeds yearly, making them the perfect training crop to save seeds.

Plant	How to Save Seed
Peppers	• Allow the fruit to remain on the plant • Pick the fruit and open it. • Remove the seeds and place them paper towel until dry.
Beans and peas	• Keep the pods on the plant until they • They are ready to be picked once th the seeds rattle within. It can take up to a • After the pods are picked, allow for drying before shelling. Alternatively, the s dry pods until the next planting season.
Tomatoes	• Once the fruit is fully ripe, scoop out they are covered in. • Add this mixture to a jar of water twice a day. • Continue to do this for five days as Any seeds that sink to the bottom can growing season. • Allow seeds to dry on some towel pa

When collecting seeds, remember that some plants are biennials, which will only create seeds in their second year of life.

Any seeds collected should be placed in an air-tight container. These containers should be clearly labeled with the date of collection and type of seeds. These seeds should ideally be stored away from direct sunlight and heat in a cool area of 32–

41° F. All stored seeds should be used within a year of collection. The older the seeds, the less chance it has of germinating.

CHAPTER 4:
LIVESTOCK

Before you consider bringing livestock onto your property, weigh your options carefully. You need to plan on having livestock and incorporate what you want into the planning phase of your homestead. However, it isn't necessary to have them brought onto the property immediately. When you have livestock, you need to be prepared to spend the money to buy them shelter, feed, transport, and any medical care they may need. Raising livestock is expensive, and sometimes it may just be cheaper to purchase what animal products you want and need. However, if you are willing to pay the cost of what your livestock may need, then go for it.

There are a variety of mammals, poultry, and even insects you can have working on your homestead. When choosing the right animal, think about why you need it.

Some animals have multiple functions, while others only have one. Remember that you aren't running a farm; you don't need hundreds of animals. A few beginner animals are all you need to start with. You can always grow your flocks and herds later if you have the space.

Beginner Livestock

If you've ever been on a farm, you will know there are many working animals you can bring onto your homestead. Not all of these are beginner friendly. Here is a handy guide to the easiest animals to try in your first year.

Animal	Benefits and Needs
Chickens	• These animals are used for meat, egg • There are many breeds; some combination. • You will need a minimum of four-squai yard or run. In a coop, chickens need roo rounded wood. Each chicken will need perch, which shouldn't be placed over food • Coops need to have nesting boxes t chickens and eggs. • Chickens eat practically anything, a cost of commercial food by allowing them seeds, or vegetables. • Chickens are prone to predation, so be enclosed. They'll also need to be lockec • Illnesses spread quickly in close si wary of possible respiratory issues. • Keep a rooster for every 10–12 hens livestock guards and will protect the hens.
Ducks	• Similar to chickens but tend to be h friendly. • Ducks require four square feet each to • Better at keeping bugs out of yc chickens, they won't damage the plants. • They do require more feed than chicke • They are prone to predation and n area. Include a coop and a small splash p The entrance to the coop should be elevato • Ducks lay their eggs anywhere, s inside or close to the coop to encourage th • Avoid getting more than one drake (ma

Rabbits	• Various breeds can be bred for meat its fur. They also produce great fertilizer. • Rabbits don't need much space, only about two feet in height for when they stan • This mammal will eat practically any vegetation. Be wary about feeding poss Commercial pellets are great to help the ki weight before slaughter. • Meat rabbits can be slaughtered after • The does are pregnant for about a mo fairly large. Nesting boxes are a must to ke • Hutches will protect your rabbits fro roaming predators. A wire bottom will allo but can affect their feet, so check them re a nesting box to rest in and have their kits. • When rabbits are out grazing in a ya you have a large colony), ensure they c enclosures, and they have protection from • Enclosures should contain wood to their teeth in check. • The enclosures should also be plac rabbits are prone to heat stroke. • Rabbits need a lot of water. Bottle attached to the outside of the cages to pr chewing them. • The does will become aggres youngsters. • Hygiene is important with rabbits flystrike (when flies lay eggs on soiled fur).
Goats	• These animals are used for meat, milk • They can clear away brush, which ca diet. Goats will also happily eat vegetables food. • These animals require a lot of spa breed you choose. The Nigerian Dwarf g feet to be comfortable. Larger breeds will n • They like to be in pastures with the weather turns bad. They are known to b

	strong fence is needed to keep them penn • It is best to keep these animals in pair: • They have an unpredictable nature, s(young children. • They are susceptible to stomach ailm everything and will need to be dewormed y
Pigs	• Pigs are great for meat and fertilizer. • They don't require a lot of space—eigl aren't active animals. Although this will de get. • They have a bad rap for being smell) the pens are regularly cleaned; this won't t • Pigs require a lot of food; to offset the allow them to forage, and feed them any ki • These are large and strong anima through fencing when after something. El(to keep them penned. They will also need away from poor weather. • Usually, it is easiest to start with eigh and raise them for about six months befor(pork. Feeder pigs should never be bred many complications. • If you intend to breed, choose a bre(needs • Neutered males usually provide the m(
Honeybees	• The initial start-up for the hives, colo| is high, but it is worth it. • Once a hive is established, it requires gives many benefits. • Hives of bees only need access to f| water) and a shallow drinking area to preve • Bee colonies can be caught in the wild • Give this animal a skip if you're allergi(hives alone until you want to collect honey. • When collecting honey, never take (also helps to nourish the hard-working inse

I'm sure many of you are asking why cattle haven't been added to the list. That's because they're not considered beginner friendly. Cows are large animals; even a calf can injure a person when they aren't paying attention. A single cow needs as much as an acre of grazing land, two if you want to rotate feeding grounds. Too much space is needed to have a cow. Goats require far less space, and their milk is easier to digest. Cattle also need barns large enough to shelter the animal during winter and a lot of hay and water to keep them comfortable. Nothing stops you from having a cow or two, but realize you need a lot of space to keep it happy and healthy.

If you aren't sure which animal best fits your needs, take one or two from the list and begin with them. You can always sell or slaughter them and get other animals if your needs change.

Consider what the animal can bring to your homestead before making your choice. A multiple function animal is always best. Animals such as goats, pigs, and bees, can be rented out to clear the ground or pollinate fields. Angora goats and rabbits are long haired animals, whose hair can be spun to create wool, which in turn can be used to make many woolen clothing items. Lastly, any animal you bring onto your homestead needs a job, otherwise, it is only eating into your resources and money.

Protecting Livestock

As your garden needs protection, so does your livestock. Depending on where you live, many predators can kill or carry off your livestock. Most predators you will encounter include but are not limited to raccoons, hawks, bobcats, lynxes, foxes, coyotes, and larger predators such as wolves or bears.

Fencing and Shelters

Free-range animals are more at risk than those in runs and sectioned-off yards. Fences and shelters are your best bet at protecting your livestock! Shelters need roofs made of metal; this prevents animals from peeling them back. The walls will need to be made of sturdy wood to prevent them from being broken. Having doors that enclose the animals inside their shelter that can't be easily opened by predators is another way to safeguard your animals.

When it comes to fences, you're spoiled for choice. You can construct a double wire chicken wire fence with a gap of 2–3 inches to prevent raccoons from reaching into yards to try and grab your poultry. This wire fence needs to be partially buried to prevent predators from digging under it to get into the yards.

You also have the option of an electrical fence powered by solar power during the day and batteries at night. This combined with a motion-sensitive light will spook any nocturnal predator from sneaking up on your animals. To prevent an aerial attack, you can add netting over the posts that keep the fencing in place. Alternatively, you can do the same with the fishing line. This should deter hawks.

It's a good idea to clear the land around the pens and yards to prevent predators from sneaking closer or dropping in. This way, your livestock sees them and warns you, or the predators second guess coming out into the open. Ideally, animals should only wander yards during the day and be firmly locked up at night, as more predators are prowling at that time.

Livestock Guardians

You can't always rely on fencing to keep predators away, but you can rely on livestock guardians. These are animals that protect the livestock or are loud enough for you to realize you need to help your animals.

Your first choices are cats and dogs. Dogs will scare off most predators, while barn cats (not indoor cats), will manage the wild rodent population for you. Dogs can be trained to spot predatory birds and bark to scare them off. A rooster among the hens will defend the hens with his life, and they're vocal when they spot a predator.

The smell of pigs will occasionally keep some predators at bay, as their smell is the same as the aggressive wild pigs. Pig pens can surround your more vulnerable animals, or you can spread their feces around the area to ward off predators— avoid this with sick animals. Other guardians you can consider are peacocks, donkeys, or llamas. Not only are they vocal, but you can use their product on your homestead.

Traps

Many counties may require you to have a license to have traps set on your farm. If this is the case, and you have a problem animal—or several—you can hire a company to get rid of them. Most states don't allow snares as this causes an animal to suffer. Avoid using them at all costs.

Veterinary Knowledge

A sick animal is an animal that can't work. In some cases, the disease can spread rapidly through your homestead. The best way to prevent any disease from becoming a problem is to ensure your animals have good quality feed, fresh water, and a clean area to live in. However, even the cleanest environment can still be a breeding ground for disease. Luckily, there are clear signs of when animals are ill, and if you are attentive, you will notice it. Any animal that goes off its feed or feeds poorly; isn't feeling well. Call a vet to have the animal checked. Regular vet visits—especially if you are breeding animals—are a necessity. The cost is worth it to have healthy animals. It's also a great idea to brush up on what kinds of diseases your livestock can get, so you can have the necessary medicine on hand to treat them. This should be discussed with your vet, as some medicines you may not have access to.

Many things can play a role in your livestock's health, namely the weather. Ensure you know what the weather is going to do, so you can prepare your homestead for the worst. Have a plan for if you need to move your animals from your homestead to the vet, or away from a natural disaster. Each animal has a preferred way of being transported, and you need to have the necessary equipment on hand for this inevitability.

Recognizing Common Diseases

Even if you aren't a vet, you should be able to recognize some of the more common diseases that can affect your livestock and you. Here is a short list of some diseases which could make the rounds on your homestead.

Disease	Type	Symptoms
Brucellosis	Bacteria l	• Often affects cattle, sheep • Most animals won't show but if they do, the disease reproductive capability of the a • Young animals may be weak after birth. • Milk-producing animals w production. • This disease can cause and blockage of teats—and lar • It can be spread to huma symptoms. In extreme case possible.
Escherichia coli	Bacteria l	• This bacterium is common • This bacterium occurs nat but it can infect food sources comes into contact with it. • Animals and people with will get infected. • It causes diarrhea, which bloody. • Severe diarrhea can le death in animals and humans. • Prevent this disease by k clean and quarantining sick an
Ringworm	Fungal	• This disease affects she pigs. • It's spread through direct c • Some animals never s disease, while others lose ha

		have crusty or scaly skin.
Flu	Viral	• This disease affects p mostly. • Poultry shows less egg pr high mortality. • Pigs tend to go off th depressed, lying in their ┌ anything. The illness will ┌ difficulties, discharge from the coughing.
Orf virus	Viral	• Known as sore mouth infe • This disease is mostly see • Sores appear on the m Nursing ewes may develop so young feed. • There is a good recovery the sores leave scars.

Many diseases could affect all your livestock, you, or just one type of animal. When you aren't sure why an animal is ill, immediately contact your vet, so they can check the animal and treat it. If you look out for your animals, they will produce what you need them to; and be happy to live on your homestead.

CHAPTER 5: PRESERVING FOOD

Unless you are lucky and live in an area where you can have permaculture—where you can grow a food-producing garden year-round—you won't have good, if any harvests during winter. This is why you need to learn how to preserve all kinds of foods to fill your pantry for the hard times. Before there were freezers and refrigerators, our ancestors developed many ways to keep food edible for long periods. You'll need to decide which best suits your needs and pocket.

When it comes to working with food, always work hygienically. If fruits and vegetables are keeping their skins during preservation, they should be thoroughly washed before you do anything. Make sure your hands and equipment are cleaned with hot water and soap. When working with meat and other produce, ensure the raw meat never touches the same space or utensils as what is used on other foods. This is a sure way to contaminate everything you are working with. Always keep a sink of hot and soapy water so you can clean in between different foods you are preserving.

Different Preservation Methods

You'll get to a point in your gardening where you are producing more than what you can eat, and this is the perfect time to start preserving your leftover crops. There are a variety of ways to do this, as some require equipment, while others don't.

Canning is a popular way to preserve foods. All you need are many sealable jars and a water bath canner. Bottles and lids need to be sterilized and kept in hot water until you are ready to add the contents to them. Depending on the recipes you're following for canning, this content may need to be cooked first. The contents are then added to the sterile, hot jars before bubbles are removed from the contents. This can be done with a metal spoon. Only when no more bubbles are visible, add the lid and only tighten a little with your fingertips. The jars are then added to the water bath to complete the process—you'll need to follow the instructions of the equipment you're using. Once the process is complete, the jars need to cool down for at least 24 hours. Afterward, the lids can be tightened, and the jars labeled. Home canned goods can last 1–2 years but should be refrigerated upon opening. Incorrect canning methods can lead to botulism poisoning. If you see a "popped" lid, likely the contents are no longer good for eating and should be properly disposed of.

Canning is likely the most complicated way to preserve food, but luckily, it isn't the only way. Fresh foods can be sealed —vacuum sealed or sealed with wax— and stored for 1–2 weeks in the fridge. Although this method prevents any microbes from reaching the food, it doesn't stop the microbes that are already on the food. However, if this method is combined with freezing, the food can last significantly longer.

As long as containers are air-tight once placed in the freezer the contents can last indefinitely. However, the temperature needs to be below 0° F. Foods can be stored as chopped, cooked, raw, pureed, or whole. It's vital to keep frozen food sealed, for if it comes into contact with the cold, dry air, this can result in freezer burn. Freezer burn changes the consistency and taste of food, causing many people to rather throw damaged food out. This isn't the only problem with freezers. You never know if the power was knocked out for an extended period before coming back on. Sometimes you come back to spoiled food, other times frozen, spoiled food, but you'll never know until you want to prepare something from your freezer. To see if your freezer has failed at any point, freeze a container with water in it, then place a coin on it. Check this coin often. As long as the coin is above the frozen liquid, you'll know that the freezer's power has remained stable.

Cooking with high levels of salt (brining) or sugar is another form of preservation. Jams and jellies are nothing more than fruit cooked with sugar or syrup to displace as much water with sugar. These mixtures are cooked to a gel-like consistency, which sets when added to water. When bottled correctly, these mixtures can last for a year or more. However, once opened, they should be consumed within two weeks to a month.

Not all microbes are bad though. When fermenting foods to get yogurt, cheese, or sauerkraut, you need specific bacteria to help you get the result you want. These microorganisms help to ferment a range of foods. Fermented foods can last up to three months, but when kept at cool temperatures they can last longer.

Although meat can be pickled or canned, most people like to salt or smoke it to increase its longevity. Smoking meat stops the growth of microbes that would spoil it. However, you will need to construct a smokehouse to achieve this. Luckily, these don't need to be very big and you can use your preferred material to smoke with (hickory, oak, etc.). The larger the smokehouse, the more meat you can smoke. Smoked meat can remain in the fridge for about four days, but up to three months in the freezer before the taste starts to change. Each type of meat you smoke has a specific duration it needs to be smoked to make it safe for consumption.

Salting is one way to dehydrate food. Once the salt is added to the food of your choice, it draws away the moisture which microbes need to ruin the food. This results in the food having a leathery appearance as seen with salted fish or jerky. Salted foods can last for 3–6 months in the fridge within an air-tight container but even longer in the freezer.

Pickling is one of the few preservation methods that don't require much equipment. All you need are jars and a pickling agent (alcohol, acid, or salt). You must work hygienically (clean jars), or you may cause food poisoning. Generally, the pickling agent is added to water and brought to a boiling point before being added to the waiting food in the jars. The lids are then added and slightly tightened before allowing the contents to cool to room temperature. Pickled foods can last in a sealed jar for 5–6 months but longer in the fridge. This duration will be dependent on the pickling recipe you are using.

Lastly is the oldest and most well-known easiest way to preserve food. Dehydration can be used for practically anything, as all you're doing is removing the liquid component of the food. This method can be combined with sealing and freezing to increase the duration of storage. There are many ways to dehydrate food, such as air drying, using a microwave (herbs), oven, or dehydrator. As this is the easiest preservation method, let's discuss it further.

Dehydration

Dehydrated foods take up much less space in comparison to other preservation methods and can be kept at room temperature. As long as no moisture gets into the storage container, the food can last for years.

Dehydrating food only removes water from it. Thus, the food retains most of its vitamins (although water-soluble vitamins will be lost), minerals, and calorie content. This method can be used for fruit, vegetables, meat, eggs, milk, full meals, and much more!

The trick with dehydrating is to get uniform dehydration. Regardless of how you decide to dehydrate your food you need to follow some rules. The food needs to be cut or spread thinly (no more than half an inch), it needs to be spaced well to allow airflow and heat through, and nothing should overlap. Overlapping thick pieces of food doesn't allow for uniform dehydration, resulting in some food having a higher water content than others.

You don't even need to dry a single type of food. You can dry different herbs in a dehydrator and then mix them to create unique blends to cook with, or even create soaps.

Dehydrators can be bought or made—if you have the know-how and tools. When buying a dehydrator, you want to balance the cost with how much power it draws and how much it can dehydrate at a time. Dehydrating can take several hours depending on what you want to dry, so this can be a drain on your electric grid. However, there are so many things you can dry with a dehydrator that it is almost worth the cost.

Food	Types
Bouillon	• Never waste food on your homeste premade food. Stews and soups take t freezer, but they don't have to when del • Spread the cooked food on a dehy and dry until the mixture is no longer tac • Cut into cubes to make bouillon blc as extra flavor to the next stew or soup

Dairy	• Milk can be dried and then powdere • Thin slices of cheese can be dried powdered.
Eggs	• When your poultry are laying too dehydrate them as well. • Scramble the eggs with your choi before adding them to a baking sheet. • Once dry, break up and add to th Roughly a teaspoon of the powder is an
Fruit	• You can dehydrate whatever yo include apples, apricots, berries, strawberries. • Don't limit yourself. If you have a grow but can buy, dehydrate that a dehydrate well, as do pineapple and kiw • Slice thinly and dehydrate for sever
Fruit leather	• One type of fruit, or a combination o and then spread thinly onto dehydrator s • Need to be dehydrated until the lea • The fruit leather can be rolled up or storing.
Meat	• All meats can be dehydrated, inclu mammalian meat. • Meat with high-fat content—suc dried but won't have a long shelf life. • All meat should be thinly slice pieces dry well and prevents spoilage th • If you are making jerky, ensure you as some recipes require you to mar dehydrating.
Vegetables	• Most vegetables can be dried with r if a vegetable requires cooking before o be cooked before dehydrating. • Many vegetables, herbs, and eve dehydrated. Try drying peppers, gar zucchinis, and tomatoes to get started.

Vegetable leather	• As with fruit leather, you can dec vegetables you want to add together be • These leather strips can make a added to stews and soups for extra flav • Try combining the vegetables wit create new and interesting flavors.

Once the food of choice is dehydrated, it must rest until it's at room temperature. Warm food tends to "sweat", and when in an enclosed space, this welcomes mold growth. Once cooled, the dehydrated food needs to be moved to an air-tight container to prevent moisture and oxygen from getting to the dried food.

Depending on what you dried, the food can last from several months to more than a year. After this, the quality of the food starts to lessen. Heat can impact the quality and affect longevity. At 60° F, dried fruit can last about a year, but as the temperature increases, the lower the quality and longevity will become. Vegetables don't last as long as fruit and will likely only last about six months before their quality gets affected.

Fruits tend to retain more water than vegetables, so you will have to condition them once they're placed in their sealable containers. Some fruit pieces may dry better than others. By adding them all into a container for 7–10 days without opening it, you can reach a uniform dryness within the container. You will need to shake the container once a day to prevent any pieces from sticking to each other. If you notice condensation on the containers that contain dried food, remove the food and dehydrate again.

Building a Solar Dehydrator

There are many brands and sizes of dehydrators on the market, but they rely heavily on electricity. If you aren't ready for that investment and you live in an area that gets plenty of sunshine, why not try to build a solar dehydrator? This dehydrator can be moved to a sunny spot in your garden and dehydrate whatever you place in it. A solar dehydrator will need to be in an area that gets at least two days of sunlight, and low humidity. Below are the instructions to make your own solar dehydrator. You can play around with the dimensions to make a bigger one. Don't be afraid to use recycled material to make it if you don't want to purchase materials. However, it is important the wood you use hasn't been treated with toxic solutions. A tip before you start construction, always pre-drill before adding screws. This prevents the wood from splitting.

Here's a list of materials and equipment you will need:

- a 2 x 4-inch plank, used for the legs. The length is determined by how tall you want the dehydrator to stand.
- a 2 x 2-inch plank. You will need several feet, depending on if you want to build braces for the legs or not. For the dehydrator, you will need at least six feet of this plank.
- an old window, or clear, hard plastic (Perspex). Needs to be ⅛ of an inch thick, measuring 20 x 23 inches.
- screen material
- heat absorbing material, such as black tarp, measuring 20 x 23 inches.
- any stretchable material (stocking) to make a drying rack.
- two hinges
- screws, roughly 1–1.5 inches, longer if connecting bracers to legs. Some may be shorted, especially when connecting the hinges.
- thermometer, to monitor the internal temperature of the dehydrator.
- hooks and string, to tie the window closed.
- thin plyboard sheet, large enough to cut all the sides of the dehydrator from.

- caulk to secure the window.
- measuring tape, table saw, and staple gun.

Dehydrator Box Sides

Measure and cut out the sides of the dehydrator box before you do anything.

- The bottom panel should be 26 ⅛ x 23 ⅙ inches. Cut six 2 x 4-inch sections out of this piece. Four of these pieces should be in the corners, while a pair should be about five inches from one of the corners. These sections are for the four legs and the two vents in the front.
- The top panel should measure 12 x 23 1/16 inches.
- Two side panels need to be cut. The longest edge (at the bottom) should measure 26 ⅛ inches, the height should be 14 ⅛ inches, and the upper edge should be 12 inches. There is a diagonal cut from the lower part of the longest edge to the upper edge which should measure roughly 20 inches.

- The back panel should be 23 1/16 by 14 ⅛ inches.

Remainder of Dehydrator

Now you are ready to put the rest of the dehydrator together.

- Cut the 2 x 4-inch lumber to the preferred length for the legs and use the 2 x 2-inch lumber to create bracing for a sturdier dehydrator. The bracer lumber should be halfway down the legs.
- Ensure the legs' spacing matches the four sections cut into the bottom panel.
- Place the bottom panel over the legs, allowing four inches of lumber above the panel. Mark this measurement on the legs.
- Cut four four-inch cleats from the remaining 2 x 2-inch lumber and drill them in place.
- Add the bottom panel to the cleats and drill in place.
- Connect the side panels to the legs above the bottom panel.

- Cut two 12-inch cleats and add them flush to the top of the side panels on the inside of the box. This will allow the top panel to rest on them.
- Add another set of cleats (12–14 inches) halfway down the side panels. This will be what you rest the drying rack on.
- Take your heat-absorbing material and staple it over the legs.
- Secure the top panel in place over the cleats on the side panels.
- Add the glass or plastic to the diagonal cut and secure it. Add some caulk if there are any gaps along the side panels.
- Add the hinges to the back and bottom panel.
- The hooks can be added to the upper part of the back panel and top panel. The string can be used to tie them together to prevent them from opening easily.

The last thing you need to do is to create the drying rack, which will slide into the dehydrator.

- Using your 2 x 2-inch lumber, create a 14 by 22 ½-inch frame.
- Stretch the stockings (or other stretchable material) over the frame.
- Keep the material taut and staple in place. Cut off excess if necessary.

Lastly, add the screen coverings to the front 2 x 4-inch ventilation sections. This will prevent insects from sneaking into your dehydrator. If you want to increase airflow, you can add a small vent in the back panel, which should also be covered with a screen.

When ready to use the dehydrator, open it and slide in the drying rack with what you want to dry. Add the thermometer close to the drying goods, so you can monitor the temperature. Close the back and ensure it seals well. Now, wait two days to see how your dehydrator works.

This is only a small dehydrator you can build to see if your region is conducive to using a solar dehydrator. Once you have determined the area is perfect, you can construct bigger and more complex dehydrators. Remember that these dehydrators may not be as precise in drying as well as what a store-bought one may be.

Root Cellars

A root cellar is a pantry outside your home that was originally used in the past to store root vegetables for winter. These cellars are kept dark and damp to increase the longevity of what is placed in them. With modern designs, this has become an effective way to stockpile a variety of foods. Food stored in root cellars can last 2–9 months, depending on the fruits and vegetables stored loosely. Other goods will last as long as their preservation methods depict. Using a root cellar is a low-cost way of storing a large quantity of food. However, note that places with higher temperatures—like the more southern states—may not get a root cellar to work.

How to Make a Root Cellar

There are a variety of ways to make a root cellar. From as easy as a barrel in the ground method to a separate cellar dug into a hill. You can even have the basement of your home as your root cellar. However, before you get ready to design a root cellar (above or below ground), there are five important factors you need to consider.

Most root cellars need to maintain a humidity of 80–95%. The high humidity prevents your stored goods from drying out. Any higher and this humidity will cause mold to grow in the cellar. Because of the high humidity, most metal objects will rust. So, if you are planning on keeping jars or cans in your root cellar, you will need to rotate them out now and again to prevent the loss of the contents. Humidity and temperature need to be monitored as they will affect what you can and can't store in the cellar.

You need good insulating material. Around the outside of a root cellar, you need to have soil. A few inches over the cellar makes for great insulation. The floor of the cellar needs to be made with soil or gravel, as this will help maintain the humidity.

There should be good ventilation once the cellar is closed—especially when storing fruit. Fruit gives off ethylene gas, which can cause other fruit and vegetables to sprout and change in texture, taste, and color. To prevent this gas from building up in the cellar you'll need a decent ventilation system. Some people like to add a window, while others add two vents. One vent should be close to the top of the cellar, allowing the ethylene gas and stale air to escape. A second pipe then comes from the top of the cellar opening up along the bottom to form a vent that brings in the fresh air. A cellar should never be without ventilation, as this can cause mold growth.

When using a window for ventilation, it must remain covered. A root cellar should always be in darkness unless you're in it.

Light can cause many types of vegetables to sprout, making them useless for consumption. If you want to lower the amount of light that gets to your stored items, you can hang burlap sacks from the shelves or placed over storage bins.

This brings us to our final important aspect of a root cellar. The shelving should best be made from rot-resistant wood (redwood, cypress, or black walnut) because the high humidity will cause most wood to rot after some time. Metal shelving conducts too much heat and will rust in the high humidity of a root cellar. Untreated wood has antimicrobial properties, which should help prevent your food from spoiling in the cellar. Different levels of shelving may give you different levels of humidity and temperature. Making the different levels perfect for storing a wide range of vegetables, fruits, jarred, and canned goods.

If you intend to have a basement that you can convert to a root cellar, this will need to be built at the same time as your house. Alternatively, you can construct your root cellar above or below ground. However, if you don't have the skills to build, it is best to consult an architect or someone who has built a root cellar before to help you with the construction.

How to Use

A root cellar needs to receive as little sun as possible. When designing one, ensure that the window and door are south facing in the northern hemisphere. You will need a thermometer and a hygrometer to measure temperature and humidity. You can get equipment that combines the two. It'll be a good idea to get several and place them around the cellar to get an accurate reading to determine where you will put what. You will also need to monitor the cellar during the winter because if the temperatures dip too low, your stored goods may freeze, damaging them.

Many vegetables can be stored in wooden boxes on shelves after they have been wiped clean of dirt. However, root vegetables such as carrots and potatoes can be stored in dirt or leaves. As long as the vegetables and fruits stored aren't wet, they won't spoil quickly.

You will need to check on your root cellar every so often to maintain the moisture of the soil. If the soil becomes dry, the humidity will lower. You can mist the air and the soil to increase humidity again. Avoid misting directly onto the open fruits and vegetables as these will become sites for mold growth.

Also, go through the boxes of stored food and remove anything that looks like it is starting to go bad. Spoiled fruit and vegetables will affect those closest to them, spreading the rot further and further into the container.

Limit the number of times you go into the root cellar. It is there to store food, not to be a fridge you can check every time you're hungry. If you have to go into the root cellar, make a list of what you may need, then take everything that is on the list. Frequent trips into the cellar will result in changes in temperature and humidity.

What Can Go Into the Root Cellar

What you put into your root cellar will be determined by the temperature and humidity you can maintain. Different fruits and vegetables store better at different temperatures and humidities. To get a rough idea of what to store under certain conditions, here is a handy table to help you.

Conditions	Fruits and Ve:
32–40° F and 90–95% humidity Cold and very moist	Beets, Brussels sprouts, (Chinese), carrots, cauliflc horseradish, Jerusalem arti leeks, parsnips, radish, rutak
32–40° F and 80–90% humidity Cold and moist	Apples, grapefruit, grapes, potatoes (38–40° F).
32–35° F and 60–70% humidity Cool and dry	Garlic and onions.
32–50° F and 60–70% humidity Cool and dry	Dry beans, peppers (dried),
50–55° F and 60–75% humidity Warm and dry	Pumpkins and winter squash
>50° F and 80–90% humidity Warm and moist	Tomatoes and sweet potatoe

Although you can store fruits and vegetables in the same root cellar, it is best to keep them separated. Have dedicated shelves for fruit in one section of your root cellar and the other section for vegetables. Because the fruit tends to give off more ethylene, place them close to a vent.

Nothing stops you from storing other fruits and vegetables in your root cellar. You may have to be a little more observant of what they may do while in the cellar. Jot anything you learn down in your notebook. By doing this you learn how long different crops last compared to others.

The cellar is also perfect for keeping your jarred foods, as by being out of the direct sunlight, their color remains unchanged. The cooling effect of the cellar will also allow canned and jar food to be stored for longer, plus, they don't take up space in your kitchen pantry.

CHAPTER 6: FIRST AID

Self-sufficiency is more than just having shelter, food, water, and energy. It is about looking after yourself in every way possible. One of which is your health. The further away from medical assistance, the more you need to be able to treat injuries and illnesses.

Why It's Necessary

Having first aid knowledge, you'll be able to deal with all minor injuries and illnesses. By increasing your first aid level —there are three—you can even manage minor to more serious injuries. First aid training allows you to remain calm in the worst situations and deal with whatever comes your way. Besides first aid courses, you can take other trauma courses to teach you to handle serious situations, such as applying stitches, or realigning bones. It's a good idea to have all your family members trained in basic first aid at the very least, in case something happens to you.

Along with this knowledge, you'll be able to stock your first aid kit for your homestead. These kits are commercially sold in most pharmacies, but they may not contain everything you need. Once you purchase a kit, you should open it up and get familiar with what is in it, and what it may potentially still need. A typical first aid kit will contain

- Bandages of various sizes and shapes. You may even have some pressure bandages.
- Different sized adhesive plasters for small cuts and abrasions.
- Gauze that is used to stem the blood flow.
- Antiseptic wash to clean wounds.
- Emergency blanket to keep a patient warm when in shock.
- Miscellaneous tools such as scissors, tweezers, antiseptic wipes, and safety pins.
- Gloves and CPR mouthpiece to help with hygiene.
- A first aid manual to remind you of what you must do.

Commercial kits are nowhere near what you need on your homestead. Think about the possible injuries and illnesses that may befall you and your family. Then add the following

- splints
- antiseptic or antibacterial cream
- pain medication (Ibuprofen or paracetamol)
- fever medication (aspirin or Tylenol)

- burn dressings (serious burns), or aloe vera (less serious)
- hot and cold compresses (usually one use only)
- anti-diarrheal medication
- electrolytes
- moleskin for blisters

You will also need to add specific medication if someone in your home has a chronic affliction. This may be EpiPens for all allergies and an asthma pump. You can even include natural remedies that you know work. No one first aid kit will be the same as another. You are in charge of filling your kit with the essentials you'll need.

A first aid kit isn't something you buy and then forget. Medications should be checked yearly to ensure they haven't expired, and anything used should be replaced as soon as possible. Your kit should be in an accessible place that everyone can reach. Making it visible means even visitors will know where it is when looking for it.

The last thing you need to remember with first aid is that you're not a doctor. If an injury is more than what you can handle, you should stabilize the patient as much as possible. Once the patient's life is no longer in danger, you can call for help. Never leave a patient unattended for long, if you can help it.

Common Injuries And Illnesses

There are many ways you can get injured on your homestead as you work the ground or move from one place to another. Here are a few possibilities and how to treat them if they happen to you. Remember that when treating someone or yourself, you must wear protective gloves and work as hygienically as possible. This not only protects you from potential diseases, but it can prevent infection from spreading. It's also your job to keep the patient as calm as possible to prevent shock from setting in.

Cuts

When working with sharp objects, you're going to get cut. It's only a matter of time. Luckily, treating cuts is straightforward.

- Start by assessing the wound. Shallow cuts and abrasions can be washed of debris and left open to the air after washing with soap and water. Deeper cuts will require more work.
- Apply pressure to the wound with gauze. Don't remove this gauze but add more on top of what you're using until the bleeding stops.
- Once the bleeding has stopped, run clean water over the wound, as this should help dislodge any debris left behind. Wash the area around the wound with soapy water to clean it. Avoid getting soap in the wound.
- If debris remains lodged in the wound, use tweezers to remove it. When debris can't be removed or is too painful to remove, it is best to get the patient to a doctor.
- Apply a thin layer of antiseptic cream to the wound to lower the

chances of infection.

- Cover the wound with gauze and keep it in place with a bandage. These dressings should be cleaned at least once a day, more if they get soiled.
- When changing dressings, note the condition of the wound. Signs of infection will include redness, swelling, and pus formation. The wound will need to be cleaned again if this occurs. If you cannot control the infection, you may need to take the patient to a doctor.

After suffering a deep cut, the patient must get a tetanus injection if they haven't had one in the last five years. Tetanus leads to lockjaw which is fatal. When applying pressure and the bleeding doesn't stop after 15 minutes, or if it's spurting, you need to get medical assistance quickly. Instruct your patient to apply pressure while you contact an emergency number. The location of the cut may also force you to see a doctor. These locations include the face, neck, joints, groin, abdomen, and chest.

Broken Bones

Broken bones can be caused by a fall or an impact on something. All broken bones should be treated by doctors. It's your job to stabilize the break as much as possible before getting medical assistance.

Signs of a broken bone are disfigurement of a limb or digit, swelling in the area of the break, bruising, and severe pain when moving or when pressure is applied to the area. If you suspect a broken back or neck, keep the patient unmoving and call for help.

There are different ways a bone can break. The most shocking is an open break, as this is when a bone tears through the skin. Before you can treat the injury, you will need to stop the bleeding. Don't apply pressure where the bone is protruding. Apply gentle pressure around the wound to stop the bleeding.

Unless you have been trained to realign bones, don't even try! Numerous blood vessels can be severed—depending on the bone you're realigning—leading to internal bleeding and a bigger problem than you can deal with on your homestead.

- You will need to immobilize the affected area with a splint. Fingers and toes can use SAM splints—or Popsicle sticks—while arms and legs will need longer splints. If you don't have these splints available, you can bind legs, fingers, and toes to their neighbor, while arms can be bound to the chest.
- Pad splints with gauze or clothing to lower the pressure on the injury. Tie the splints in place above and below the break.
- Apply an ice pack to the swollen area—or around an open fracture—to help with the pain and swelling. Never apply an ice pack directly to the skin. It's best to wrap it in some cloth to protect the patient's skin.
- Broken bones are painful, and there is a chance your patient may go into shock. This needs to be managed, as it can be fatal.

- Symptoms of shock include feeling faint and having shallow, rapid breathing. Have the patient lie down with their head a little lower than the rest of the body. You can also lift the legs by a foot to help get blood flow back to the brain. However, if you suspect a back or neck injury, don't move the patient at all! Also, don't lift any leg that is broken.

Broken bones can be severe enough that a person's body goes into shock and stops breathing. You shouldn't leave their side if you can help it, as you may have to perform CPR.

Concussion

A concussion is caused when the head takes a hard blow, resulting in a potential injury to the brain. Not all head traumas cause concussions, but all concussions come from head traumas. When someone suffers a blow to the head, it generally won't develop into something that some pain medication and an ice pack can't fix. However, head trauma is tricky, one minute your patient will be fine, and the next they may be suffering from seizures. Luckily, there are some tell-tale signs of a bump being more severe than it first appears. If your patient suffers from

- bleeding from the nose or face
- leaking clear fluid from the nose or ears
- has a severe headache that won't go away
- poor balance
- unequal pupil size
- vomiting
- slurred speech
- seizures

Then they likely have a concussion. Children will exhibit all these symptoms but will also be crying uncontrollably, refusing to eat, and repeatedly vomiting. Babies will show swelling in their soft spots. If your patient exhibits any of these signs, get medical assistance.

- Treat all head wounds as serious until proven otherwise.
- Keep the patient as still as possible while elevating the head and shoulders—unless you suspect a neck injury.
- Gently apply pressure to the point of impact if it is bleeding. Don't press too hard, as you can't be sure of a cracked skull.
- Monitor your patient for 24 hours (48 hours for children) and allow paracetamol to be taken as pain relief.

There is no reason to keep a person with a non-serious head injury awake. Allow them to sleep but check on them periodically to see if you can rouse them. When a patient falls into unconsciousness, get medical assistance.

Animal Attacks

When working on a homestead, there's a good chance you'll get bitten by your menagerie at some point. As long as your animals are up to date with their rabies vaccinations, you only need to treat a bleeding wound. However, you will need to be more cautious with wild animals. An unprovoked attack by a wild or feral animal is usually a sign of rabies. When attacked by a wild animal, you should defend yourself. Do this by getting to a protected area (don't run, this can trigger the hunting instinct in predatory animals), defending yourself with what is in your reach, or dispatching the animal. Once it is safe to do so, treat any injuries left by the animal.

- When you know the rabies status of the animal is negative and the injury is minor (barely broken skin and scratches), all you need to do is wash the wound with soap and water. Then apply antiseptic cream and monitor the wound as it heals.

- When the rabies status of the animal is unknown, or the injury is jagged or has deep punctures, the injury is considered severe and in need of emergency treatment. Injuries to the face, joints, neck, hands, and feet need to be treated by a medical professional.
- Apply pressure to the wounds and treat the same as a deep cut. The patient will need to get to a doctor as soon as possible to get a rabies injection.

Rabies is a fatal disease; this is why we immunize our animals against it. If an unknown animal is acting strange, avoid it at all costs and contact emergency services to get further instructions. When bitten by a potentially rabid animal, try to remember as many details about it as possible, as this will help professionals hunt it down before it can attack anyone else.

Even if the animal doesn't prove to be rabid, animal bites carry serious repercussions, even if it's your pet. The bite will introduce many kinds of secondary bacterial infections that can lead to infections and even gangrene. Treat all animal bites as serious.

Diarrhea

Diarrhea can either be due to bacterial or viral infections. Most people are affected by this disease at least once in their lifetime. The symptoms are easy to recognize. If you or your patient are suffering from the following symptoms, then likely you and they have diarrhea:

- painful abdominal cramps
- bloat
- nausea and potential vomiting
- fever
- loose bowels, which can become bloody over time

As the disease runs its course, you or the patient may have low energy, feel weak, have a low appetite, and have a headache brought on by the dehydration caused by the loose bowels. Diarrhea is your body's way of expelling something that shouldn't be in it. The disease normally lasts a couple of days, and most of the time it should just run its course.

The best treatment for diarrhea is to take it easy by resting and drinking plenty of fluids with electrolytes to replace what the body is losing. Even if the patient's appetite is low, it's advised to consume foods high in carbohydrates and fiber, while avoiding fatty foods. Antidiarrheals can be taken to help lower the intestinal spasms, giving them a chance to reabsorb fluid, electrolytes, and nutrients.

However, if the loose bowels continue for too long, it can cause serious dehydration and even death. If diarrhea lasts longer than two days without signs of improvement, it may be a good idea to consult a doctor for the next course of action. You may have to scrutinize what you have been cooking and eating, as food poisoning can result in diarrhea.

Getting Help to You

When someone is too seriously injured to be moved you have to ensure help can get to them. This means having the road to your homestead cleared and marked. Paramedics need to be able to find your home when they are looking for you. It's wise to have a distinguishing aspect of your home or property that will allow medical assistance to spot the property more readily. If you know the coordinates of your homestead, this will be even better.

However, what happens in you are incapacitated and your children need to care for you? Ensure that the first aid kid is in an easy-to-reach place that isn't cluttered. You may also want a list of instructions on what to do either in the kit or on the fridge to help youngsters know what they should do in an emergency. Have drills and practice when you have downtime on the homestead. Everyone needs to be self-sufficient to ensure the smooth running of the homestead. It may also be a good idea to have a check-in system in place. This allows you to check up on people and for them to check up on you.

Natural Remedies

Before there were medications in pill form, natural remedies were used to aid in all manner of ailments. These remedies still exist today, and depending on what you have on your homestead, you can recreate and use them. There are thousands of natural remedies and recipes online. Most of these will help with ailments you usually treat with over-the-counter medications. By keeping some handy natural remedies on hand, you can manage many illnesses without needing to go to a doctor. However, please realize that natural remedies cannot replace doctors and medications for serious diseases. Before relying on a natural remedy to cure a persistent ailment, discuss its use with your doctor.

Treating Diarrhea

There are a wide variety of mint species used to help with many of the symptoms of diarrhea. The leaves can be added fresh or dried to a boiled cup of water and drunk after 5–10 minutes. The liquid helps lower the spasms in the intestines and helps with abdominal pain. Mint is easy to grow in a container, and you only need a few leaves to feel better.

Alternatively, you can use rice water. Cook your rice of choice halfway, then strain the liquid. Allow this to cool down and drink it. Not only will it make a gentle drink on your stomach, but it lowers the duration of suffering diarrhea.

Treating Nausea

You can never go wrong with ginger when it comes to nausea. Although ginger can only be grown in the hardiness Zone 9 and up, it can be found in local supermarkets. The candied variety can work for nausea, but it's best to get it fresh to make a tea from it. You'll need at least half an inch of fresh ginger per two cups of tea you make.

- Grate the ginger and add it to a volume of two cups of freshly boiled water.
- Allow the ginger to sit in the water for 5–10 minutes.
- Strain the liquid and add some lemon or honey to taste.

The tea can be drunk hot or cold, whatever your preference is.

Treating Bug Bites

Nothing is quite as irritating as an itchy bug bite! Luckily, there are many ways to deal with it. A dab of chamomile solution is the go-to for most people; however, not everyone has this in their home. If your homestead has clay, you can add a little of it directly to the bite. This eases the pain, itchiness, and swelling. Another way to deal with these bites is to use a warm metal spoon. After stirring your tea, lightly apply the spoon to the bite. Most of the itchiness should vanish after a minute.

Treating Sore Throats

A sore throat is detrimental, and people long for some relief from it. There are many ways to deal with a sore throat, from throat lozenges to hot toddies. However, if you have bees, you have a chance to make your own sore throat treatment. Honey, cinnamon, and turmeric have been used for centuries because of their antibacterial properties. The combination of the three is a great way to deal with a sore throat.

You will need one teaspoon of honey to half a teaspoon of cinnamon or turmeric —or both if you are so inclined. The spices should be mixed well into the honey before it's swallowed. This allows the mixture to coat the throat. However, if you can't stomach this idea, stir the combination into a cup of boiling water. Drink it as soon as the honey is completely dissolved.

Treating Boils or Splinters

Boils and splinters can be a nuisance to remove from your skin. Before you reach for a pin to lance a boil or remove a splinter, consider using a potato. A potato poultice has been used for ages to deal with these nuisances.

To treat a boil, grate the potato and apply it as a poultice to the affected area with gauze and a bandage. Keep it in place for 4–8 hours, replacing the poultice as needed. After this time has elapsed, open the area for 4–8 hours to breathe. Keep applying the poultice until the boil disappears.

For a splinter, apply the grated potato for 24 hours, adding a fresh poultice every 4–8 hours. This will help to lower the pain, and swelling, and bring the splinter to the surface. You can also use bicarbonate of soda paste to do the same thing.

Treating Painful Muscles

Working on a homestead is difficult and you're likely to suffer sore muscles from time to time. There are many products you can use to ease this pain, but why buy something you can make? All you need is some cayenne powder and coconut oil.

- Take a cup of coconut oil and add to a saucepan over low heat.
- Add three tablespoons of cayenne powder.
- Stir the two ingredients until they are well mixed in a liquid form.
- Continue to stir for five minutes.
- Remove from the heat and pour into a clean, sealable container.
- Allow the mixture to cool to room temperature and solidify. If it doesn't solidify at room temperature, add it to the fridge.

The next time you strain a muscle, take some of the ointment and rub it into your skin. It will burn a little, but no more than any other muscle cream. Be wary of touching your eyes after you use the cream. Cayenne contains capsaicin, as with all chili species, and it'll burn sensitive mucus membranes.

Treating Migraines

Remember how I mentioned growing herbs and flowers benefits you and your garden? Lavender is one of those reasons. Pick a few sprigs and add them to your shower to help with migraines. You can even add some of the dried leaves to a tiny pillow or herb bag you keep close to your bed. The leaves and flowers can even be added to a tea. Drink it when you feel a migraine coming on.

Communication

Nowadays, we take for granted that we can easily communicate with the rest of the world. Communication with the rest of the world is vital, especially in an emergency. Rural areas won't necessarily have landlines available. In some areas, you may be lucky to have cell service coverage, but most of the time, in very rural areas, you might not. Most cell phones work best the closer you are to a cell tower, something which doesn't exist in most areas where people want to have a homestead. Luckily, you have some options for communication available to you.

Satellite internet and phones may be pricey, but they will ensure you have access to the internet and people outside of your homestead. Some satellite phones even allow you to communicate with video, though most will only do calls or text messages.

Your other options are radios or walkie-talkies. Modern walkie-talkies can communicate up to 36 miles. However, the further you want to communicate, the more expensive the product becomes. The advantage of walkie-talkies is that they can be used anywhere on your homestead, which is great if you have a family member somewhere on the property, and you want to know where they are. You can even give one to your closest neighbor, in case you or they ever need help. Unfortunately, even though they can reach farther distances, their signal can be influenced by the lay of the land. Although they are cheaper than a satellite phone, they aren't as reliable.

CHAPTER 7: HOW TO MAKE MONEY

Although you may need less money while on your homestead, you cannot avoid it completely. Not everything you need can be traded or bartered for; sometimes cold hard cash is needed. Tax, farm equipment, and animal feed are just some of the items you need money for. Luckily there are many ways for you to make money. You have worked hard to have your homestead, and now it's time that it works and earns money for you. Your homestead may already be generating multiple streams of income that you aren't aware of yet.

Earning Money

How you make money on a homestead comes down to what you have on it and how creative you are. Remember to follow all the regulations needed for the sale of live animals, animal products (milk, honey, and meat), and cooked or baked goods. There is likely a chance you will have to pass a health inspection before you are allowed to sell premade food to other people.

Before selling any of the products from your homestead, it's a good idea to create a label and name for yourself. Ideally, you want to advertise your homestead with the label on your products. Think of something creative and eye-catching. You're not the only person trying to make money from their homestead. You need to stick out from the competition. The products you produce can be sold on your homestead property, at a farmer's market, or even as part of a community-supported agriculture group. Selling your goods may seem daunting at first, but you will improve the more you do it.

Plants

Any excess fruits and vegetables you can't store, or preserve are a great way to make extra money. When you purchase animal feed that comes in burlap sacks, these can be converted into unique tote bags. When people purchase many products from you, they will be pleased to see highly decorated and colorful bags they can also purchase to make their loads easier to carry. These bags will also do well at craft markets or even placed online if you want an online store.

Many people love the idea of receiving fresh flowers but often balk at the prices they have to pay. By growing a patch of unique and beautiful flowers, you can have clients choose what they want and make their own bouquet.

Dried herbs sell surprisingly well to hobbyists as they use them in making their own creations. You can grow and dry these herbs for them, or you can use them to create unique combinations for salves, tinctures, or natural remedies. If you know medicinal herbs, you can grow these too and create ready-to-use teas for many ailments. Even if you don't know about medical herbs, it's worthwhile learning about the different kinds there are.

As you collect seeds every year, you may find some plants perform better and produce far more than you need. Unique cultivars will get snapped up by home growers and other homesteaders who are starting. Be sure that the seeds are labeled correctly, and mention if they are heirloom or not. Get creative with drawings on your seed packets to attract more customers.

Seeds aren't the only way you can make money though. Consider growing garlic within the first year of starting your homestead. Good-looking garlic bulbs are well sought after as this vegetable takes months to grow. When growing garlic from seed, it can take a year or longer to grow, and then it still needs to make a fleshy bulb. Selling the cloves or whole bulbs saves people much time and effort and puts some money in your back pocket.

You can even grow specialty crops to match the time of year. Jack-o-lantern pumpkins are great for carving and the Halloween spirit. Make harvesting fun by allowing people to choose the exact pumpkin they want.

While you are growing your garden, consider starting a small nursery. Saplings and transfers are easier to grow than seeds. By having a wide range of trees, bushes, berries, flowers, and vegetables, your customers can pick and choose what they want to plant. These nurseries don't need to be very large, and all you need to make it work are pots of various sizes. Choose plants that are easy to grow or propagate. Strawberries are a great fruit to propagate, and there is so much you can do with the fruit. Even if the plants in your nursery don't sell, you can use them in your garden!

When a homestead has woodland attached to it, there is a great opportunity to forage and sell what you find. Many edible mushrooms and fruits can be found. However, when foraging, be sure that you can identify the plants and mushrooms you collect, as some can cause digestive problems and even death!

Do you have maple, birch, or walnut on your property? If so, teach yourself how to tap and make syrup! Tapping usually occurs during February and March, but this will depend on where you are and the temperatures you experience. Tapping should only be done to trees that have a diameter of at least 10–12 inches at your chest height. Unique tree saps can be tastier than honey if you make them correctly.

Animals

With enough chickens and ducks, you are likely to see a stage when you have too many eggs to store, cook, or bake with. Sell off the excess. Many people like the idea of free-range eggs. With a drake and rooster about, you can even sell fertilized eggs to people who want to hatch their own fluffy chick or duckling. If you have a particularly rare breed of poultry, you may have clients around the country begging to buy these eggs. Be sure to learn the correct packaging for these living eggs. You will also need to brush up on any laws surrounding the shipping of live animals and eggs. Alternatively, people can buy chicks and ducklings from you. You can sell them as young as a day old! You may need an incubator to ensure a better hatch rate than what hens can.

Bees create a treasure trove of products you can sell. The first thing people think of when you say bees, is honey. However, you can also collect the honeycomb to get their wax. This wax can be used in salves, candles, and even soaps.

Angora goats and rabbits need grooming to keep their hair under control. This hair can be spun into wool and then sold. Alternatively, you can keep the wool and use it for other projects. This brings us to animal pelts. If you are already slaughtering rabbits for your meat consumption, you can save the pelts and tan them. Many hobbyists would happily take a well-tanned pelt to create mittens, socks, and so much more. You can even keep the pelts and make clothes to sell.

Not all states allow the sale of raw milk, but if you're in a state that does, then great. Excess milk from cattle and goats can be sold off or used in the making of dairy products such as butter, cheese, and yogurt.

Your animals can work for you. Goats and pigs can clear brush away, and if you have a particularly rare breed in the area, people may request you stud it out. You likely have a male cow, goat, pig, or rabbit on your farm if you are breeding for meat or milk. If this is a registered stud, you can rent the animal out to help other homesteaders breed their animals. Though, if this is something you want to try, it is advised that you have the animal insured against possible injury it may sustain while it isn't on your property.

While on the subject of breeding; a good livestock guardian is something many people need. Breeding guardian dogs is one way to ensure good genes are passed along. However, you should be a responsible breeder and follow all the regulations surrounding the breeding and selling of animals. Have the animals frequently checked by a vet to ensure their health throughout the pregnancy.

Animals produce a lot of manure. Take the time to compost it correctly, as many gardeners like to use farm compost to better their gardens. Those excess feed bags are the perfect container for compost.

Living broiler animals can be sold, or if you're licensed to slaughter, you can provide meat at the market. However, be aware that your abattoir needs to be inspected, to ensure it is up to code.

Creativity

Tap into your creative side. Do you have some pieces of wood lying around that can't be used in a project? Make wooden ornaments, spoons, markers, whatever you can imagine. Decorate them to make them eye-catching and see if they catch anyone's eye. Never allow a usable item to be thrown out. Something as simple as a broken pallet can be transformed into furniture, raised beds, or markers.

Learn to make soap and create combinations with herbs and fruits to make unique fragrances. Packaging sets of similar products will make them more dazzling and attract people to your stall. You can even sell baked and preserved goods! With wool from your animals, you can create gloves, hats, baby booties, and more. You're only limited by your imagination.

Sell an Experience

Once you have an orchard and perhaps a berry patch, sell the experience of picking food on a homestead. Many city people love the idea of coming to the country to enjoy something as simple as picking an apple. You can even train young people who want to start their own homestead by having them stay on your homestead and working the land. This idea is best for more established homesteads, but it could be a goal you can work toward.

Your Knowledge

With the internet, you can have a steady income from the comfort of your own computer. When you aren't working on your homestead, there are many things you can do in your downtime. Blogs and vlogs about your adventures on the homestead are one way to generate an audience, especially when you are using YouTube to advertise your adventures.

How-tos about getting a homestead set up are becoming very popular as more and more people are looking for ways to get off the grid, grow their own food, or raise farm animals. Recording your victories and struggles will show your audience what you and, in turn, they are capable of.

You can even use the internet to get a part-time, online job. Many places are looking for online teachers, editors, and even writers. Freelance writing about topics you enjoy is a great way to make money after a long day of working on the homestead.

How To Save Money

It isn't just about making money on your homestead. It's about how far you can stretch what you have and still put away some for the future. An emergency fund is a must-have on a homestead because you never know what the future can hold. The best way to save money is to learn to budget. You have already created a budget to move onto your homestead, so it shouldn't be too difficult to create one while living on it. With a budget, you can prevent yourself from spending too much or getting involved in too many projects.

Learn to adapt to a zero-waste lifestyle. If something breaks, fix it. This may be difficult at first if you don't have the necessary skills, but these skills are essential. Fixing clothes, toys, and even heavy equipment on your farm will prevent you from wasting money on buying something new when something can be fixed. Use what you have for as long as you can and fix it at the first sign of a problem. Never put off a repair job that can be dealt with now. If fixable and you don't know how, look for aid or learn how to fix it. One way to lower the wear and tear of an item is to only use it for its intended purpose.

Sometimes something is beyond fixing. This is okay. Old clothes can be torn into strips and used to clean instead of paper towels. Old equipment, such as tractors that become unfixable, can be sold for scrap or specific parts. Never throw it out; you'll be surprised who may want it.

The same goes for food. Many people have leftovers in their fridges; some will leave them to grow mold, while others eat them. Be the kind of person that doesn't waste a single meal. Most meals are safe to eat 3–5 days after being cooked. If you don't get to it, that's fine! Pigs make great garbage disposals, but if you don't have pigs then compost the leftovers.

Avoid buying brand new items if possible. There are many fine secondhand options for tools and clothes that are still of good quality. Estate sales are a great way to get second-hand tools!

When it comes to things you have to buy, consider buying in bulk, especially for things you know you'll be using on your farm for years to come. The excess can be stored, but will always be available, without you having to go to the store for it.

Get creative when it comes to making items instead of buying them. Something as necessary as a multi cleaner is cheaper to make in the long run than buying it. Many of these homemade cleaners are gentler than commercial cleaners. This way, once in the greywater, the water can still be used for your garden safely. You'll need the following items to make it:

- a cup of vinegar
- a tablespoon of Sal Suds (biodegradable cleaner)
- three cups of water
- about 10 drops of orange essential oil
- about 10 drops of grapefruit essential oil
- a 32-ounce glass bottle with a plastic spray nozzle

To make the spray

- Add all the ingredients to the bottle.
- Add the nozzle and shake to mix the ingredients.

Now you have a ready-to-use multipurpose cleaner that can be used on plastic, wood, and metal surfaces. Be wary of using this cleaner on surfaces such as tile or granite, as after some time the acidic mixture can start to dissolve it. You don't even have to limit yourself to a citrus scent. Play around with peppermint essential oil if you prefer the smell.

Take the time to look around your home right now to see what items can be made or gotten rid of. You may even surprise yourself with what you can get rid of—as it has no place on a homestead—and what you can learn about yourself.

CONCLUSION

Anyone can move to a homestead, but not everyone has the grit to see it through. Homesteading is the art of becoming self-sufficient away from what many people believe are the comforts of the modern world. However, this isn't true. A well-planned and managed homestead can have all the comforts of your home right now.

Energy needs are met by either remaining on the grid or using alternative power such as solar, wind, or water. You can grow fruits and vegetables and raise livestock. There are even a wide variety of ways to get water to your home. You can even decide what kind of house you want to live in. As long as you research the laws in the area where you want to live, starting a homestead is possible for everyone. It's by no means an easy task, but it's far more rewarding than a 9–5 job. What other job allows you the same freedoms as homesteading?

The perfect homestead starts with a plan on paper. By drawing up a plan of action, a budget, and listing your goals, you get a rough idea of what you need to do on your homestead to not only survive but thrive! Once you have your goals in mind, you need to find that perfect piece of land to call your own. Land may not be easy to come by, but with enough searching and luck, you'll find what you need. Be sure to look up any possible laws that can stand in your way of making the perfect homestead, especially if you want to leave the various grids.

You want a piece of land that's big enough to fulfill all your needs but not too big to manage by yourself or with your family. Ideally, you want a property that gives you access to mineral and water rights as this will make your life significantly easier.

Once you have your land, start to develop it with your goals in mind. Do you want a garden or multiple? What kind of livestock do you want to keep? All these questions should be part of the goals you put down on paper earlier.

Consider the climate and hardiness zone to choose the best plants to give you the best yields, as this will determine how much food you can produce. Don't be afraid of producing too much over the growing season. There are many ways to preserve the food for the coming colder months when you struggle to grow anything.

One way to continue to get food during these cold months is to keep livestock. These animals can provide meat, eggs, milk, and even wool or pelts. However, when you have animals on your farm, you need to care for them. They also need food, water, and shelter. Animals that wander are animals that get eaten. Protective runs and yards prevent predators from getting to your animals. You can also deter predators by keeping some livestock guardians on hand.

Depending on where your homestead is, your closest doctor may not be close at hand. Learning first aid ensures you can heal minor injuries and stabilize the severe injuries long enough to get your patient, or you, to a doctor. Don't dismiss natural remedies as things of the past. Many medications today use the active ingredients in plants for more effective healing. Something as simple as a cup of mint tea can help with diarrhea, while ginger tea can settle nausea.

While a homestead can cost a lot of money to get started, once it's functioning, you can use it to make some extra money. Sell off excess produce and animals or share your knowledge with the world about how you started your new home. There is always someone willing to pay for farm fresh goods. Once on a homestead, you may not be making as much money as you were in the city. Don't fret! You already established a budget to get your homestead, apply that same knowledge to create a living budget. You will soon realize that you don't have to buy everything you used to, especially when you learn how to mend clothes, farm equipment, and more.

Anyone can homestead, but not everyone is prepared to move away from the comforts they have come to expect from living on the grid. Perhaps you're someone who wants to lower their carbon footprint and want to learn some homesteading skills to achieve this. Urban homesteading is possible, and many people practice it. If you're not ready for the move to a rural homestead, apply what knowledge you have learned in this book to create a small backyard homestead. You can also supplement your energy needs with solar panels. You can even offset your grocery bill by growing your favorite vegetables and fruit in a raised bed. *Homesteading is about being self-sufficient, not living in the middle of nowhere.*

You now have the basic knowledge of getting ready to have a homestead. Take the time to do extra research to ensure you know the full extent of the laws in the area you want to live. There is nothing else stopping you from making the move to a homesteader lifestyle, even if it's to just plant a vegetable garden this year. You have nothing to lose by making small changes to make yourself self-sufficient. Get up and seize the opportunity before you, and happy homesteading!

Printed in the USA
CPSIA information can be obtained
at www.ICGtesting.com
LVHW022346041224
798370LV00009B/188

9781806317257